PRANKS
The Guide To Dirty Tricks & Practical Jokes

by
Devious Dennis

DORRANCE PUBLISHING CO., INC.
PITTSBURGH, PENNSYLVANIA 15222

The Dirty tricks and practical jokes described in this book are meant for the reader's entertainment and enjoyment only. Common sense would caution the reader not to perform any dirty tricks or practical jokes that would cause undue harm, injury, or loss to any individual or business.

Please practice safe fun!

Copyright © 1993 by Devious Dennis
All Rights Reserved
ISBN # 0-8059-3349-2
Manufactured in the United States of America

Second Printing

Dedication

To my bizarre family that taught me that being different is unique, and especially to my zany mom that started me pranking

Table of Contents

Introduction vi
1. Pranks 1
2. My Next Book 143
3. Getting Rich 144
4. Ordering Information 145

Introduction

At last we can come out of the closet and unite! (Maybe I should use a different phrase; I may give people the wrong idea.) It's time for practical jokers to join together and take over the world. Well, not quite. We can do our devious deeds and help the world to laugh, and society certainly needs more humor.

Pulling off pranks is really quite an art. The more you do, the better you get. When I first started my career as Devious Dennis, I was reprimanded several times. However, the more I tried my tricks, the better I got, and more ideas were created by my devious mind. I wrote my book in a special way to help you, the reader, learn and get ideas. Many categories are interchangeable but are design that way purposely, to stimulate your reading. Your thorough reading will help you to create your own pranks through the studious application of mine. Naturally, I couldn't print every prank I've done, and I have tried to keep it as clean as possible. There are many dangerous pranks to pull, but we should avoid them; the whole idea is to have a good time. Some of the practical jokes may seem awkward, odd, or dirty to you, but once you get started, they get easier.

If you are shy and can't get started when with a group, just try the old tap on the shoulder of a friend opposite you and play innocent. By the time you finish this book, you will be qualified to wear the Devious Dennis Stamp.

Someday I see April Fool's Day being changed to Devious Dennis Day. As a matter of fact, we should make it a national holiday–write your congressperson!

A

Affairs

I had several affairs one summer, and I told Charlie, a fraternity brother, about my escapades. Charlie was twenty years older and kept bugging me to set him up with one of my girls. I agreed to let him use my apartment and to set him up with a horny broad. But what he didn't realize was that I had gone to a gay bar and paid a homosexual man fifty dollars to dress up as his date. I introduced them at a bar, gave Charlie my apartment keys, and said, "Have fun." I secretly followed them back; I had a tape recorder hidden in the bedroom. I waited outside. It took only six minutes for Charlie to come running out in hysterics and squeal his tires for home. When I heard the tape recording, I laughed even more. Oh, by the way, Charlie wouldn't speak to me for two months, but it was worth it. If you have a friend who thinks he's a Romeo, set him up with a gay man as a laugh. He won't boast anymore. It may appear to be an expensive prank, but I had fun each time. You will be surprised at how willing most gays, transsexuals, and transvestites are to help you out. They have the same sense of humor as heterosexuals.

Ambulances

If you ever get a chance to work for an ambulance service, do so. It's fun, and you get a good experience of what life means. These antics I pulled may seem morbid and unprofessional, but I was a dedicated medic. Medics see so much death and so many morbid experiences that they need an outlet for their emotions.

I recorded screams, chains, and anything that resembled a horror movie. I included a delay of five minutes on the tape so the sounds would not start until five minutes down the road. Our company was under contract to ten funeral homes, so we were always going to pick up a corpse. I kept the tape

recorder hidden in the car. Then, when we had gotten a death call and loaded the body in the rear end of the car, I secretly started the recorder. About five minutes later, while driving down the road, moans and groans started coming from the body as if it were haunted. My partner usually got pretty terrified. When I would have a "wet-behind the ears" trainee, he would get so scared that he would jump out of the ambulance. You might want to try this in your regular car, under the seat or in the trunk.

The young kids that came to work usually wanted just to run the red lights and sound the sirens just for noise; they really weren't impressed by the seriousness of the job. I sometimes made the new fellow ride in the back with the dead body. I told 'im it was a state law, etc. Can you imagine riding in the dark at 2:30 with a stiff? It usually had the fellows scared, and sometimes they would quit. I kept the same guys riding in the back, and when they got switched to a new partner they automatically jumped into the back of the ambulance. They sure would get embarrassed when they found out they didn't have to, that it was a joke. Had one fellow do it on a house death; it shocked the funeral directors.

Another trick you may try relates to the morgue. I was doing special duty one night at the hospital when one of my co-workers came to pick up a body for embalming. It just happened that I had my ape-man mask with me that night. As Bob came into the hospital and signed for the body's release, an orderly and I ran down to the morgue, and I went in. I took off my shirt, put on rubber gloves and my ape-man mask, and climbed onto the table with the other dead bodies. I pulled a sheet over myself and lay quietly. The orderly turned out the lights and locked me in the morgue. About five minutes later, the orderly and Bob, the ambulance driver, unlocked the door, turned on the lights, and came in. The orderly said, "The body is to the right, Bob; be careful it's diseased." Just as Bob got close to picking me up, I sat up, and the sheet fell off. When Bob saw my ugly mask, he backed up in horror until he fell against the organ refrigerator. The growling sound nearly caused Bob to faint. I laughed so hard that I fell off the table and nearly wet my pants. The orderly picked Bob up, to help him regain his composure. He had a hard time living it down.

In some areas you can rent a hearse. It could save your job or just keep it a secret from your boss, like me. Drive your hearse up to a house and take out the stretcher. Go up to the door and ask where the body is. The people at the house will be surprised when you come to pick up a dead person and there is no deceased present.

If my partner and I approached a hitchhiker on the highway, my partner got into the rear of the ambulance and pulled the death cover over himself. Then we picked up the hitchhiker. That was when the fun began.

You can also put a horror mask on the face and tell the embalmer how ugly the person is. When he takes off the cover, boy, is he shocked.

Just when you get help to lift the casket, have the "corpse" come out.

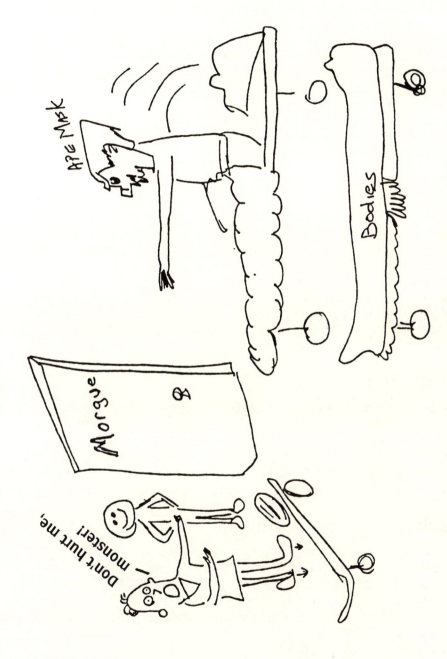

I was locked in the morgue for about ten minutes.

On first dates, I used to like to pick up the girl in a hearse. Words could not describe their expressions. I gave up using a garbage truck; the girls refused to go out with me.

Another favorite of mine was to get an old casket and have a friend get in it, then drive the hearse down the street. Have the rear door fixed so that, when leaving a stop light, the casket rolls out onto the street in front of the car behind you, causing it to stop. When you get out and try to pick up the coffin, act like it is too heavy to budge. Some courteous motorist will try to help to lift the casket back into the hearse. Just as he or she begins to lift, the person in the casket throws open the lid and screams. This is a real shocker to the victims.

Amnesia

Whoever attempts this practical joke must be able to keep a straight face and a serious attitude. I was dating Jane for about a month when I decided to pull this one off. Jane asked me to carry some books down to her basement. When she wasn't looking, I faked a terrible fall and acted like I was unconscious. When she came to my rescue, I put on my amnesia routine. I said, "Who are you? Where am I?" I didn't even know my name. I received so much love and attention that evening that I really hated to "snap out of it" and tell her the truth. I learned this routine also works while playing football or for any serious knock on the head. Good luck!

Animal Sounds

This practical joke works better in a rural community and in the summertime, when windows are open. Record some wild animal sounds, like a cougar, tiger, or lion. I always liked to use the cougar. We would turn off our car lights and pick a spot close to a house or two. Turn up the growling sounds, and the people actually think there is a wild mountain lion loose. Rumors start around the rural community, and it is almost as bad as a Big Foot scare.

Ashtrays

Although flash paper is illegal in most states, I used to leave strips in an ashtray. When someone put his cigarette down, a giant ball of fire would ignite and attract attention. It's a surprise and embarrassment to the victim.

I have also taken a bullet apart and spread the gun powder in the ashtray. The powder mixes with the ashes and can't be detected. And when the person rests his cigarette in the tray, there is a giant puff of smoke. It is a good way to get a waitress's attention.

Auto

While autos get smaller and smaller, they also get lighter. Just get four or five fellow together, pick up the car, and place it on someone's front porch. Or just pick it up and turn it around.

Ever get tired of having that certain car parked near you? Sometimes there are ads in the paper to buy junk cars; the wrecker will come and pick it up. Just dial the junkyard and give them the information. Be there to tell them you'll bring the title down later. The car is taken off your hand and out of sight. The neighbor just can't figure out what happened to it.

Another trick is to tape up the headlights of the car. The victim usually doesn't notice until it gets dark; he turns on his headlights, and it looks like they are burned out. He pulls into a service station to have them checked or new ones put in. When the attendant comes over to look it over and he or she discovers the tape, the driver really looks foolish.

While stopped at a stop light as one of the passengers, just act like you are having a convulsion. Jerk and scream and do anything to embarrass the driver. Or hide below the windows so other motorists can't see you and start singing loud and off key.

While your friend's auto is vacant, turn the radio on full-blast and turn on the wipers, heater, and all the inside gadgets. When the person returns and starts the ignition, he is bombarded with noise and moving objects. He is caught temporarily off guard.

If you want to stop the exhaust system, stuff a wad of paper in the pipe. Jam it so that no exhaust can leak out, and then the problems start.

There is also an exhaust whistle that slips over the pipe. When the car starts up, the pipe starts screaming and frightens the motorist. I usually have this on hand for weddings.

B

Babies

Whenever a baby is to be born, there is much excitement stirring for the arrival. When the baby is born, it is customary to send a baby card to the mother to congratulate the new arrival. In the gift shops, there are pictures of black and white babies on different cards. If the family is white, send them a card with a picture of a black baby on it. And if a black family, send a white baby card. Don't sign your name but someone else's name that the family knows.

When Mother's Day comes, send a card with a picture of a different race to Mom. Then sign her son-in-law's name. Or send a Mother's Day card to some man who deserves it; he'll get the point.

Banks

If the bank has ever foreclosed on your house, repossessed your car, or raised your interest fee for no reason, and you want to cause an inconvenience, follow my advice. Rent a safety deposit box and put a dead fish in it. Leave it in there forever, if you choose, and don't come back. It will really stink up the whole bank. The bank officials are not permitted to open any of the boxes themselves, so they can't trace it. In the meantime, the smell gets worse, and they lose customers.

Barrels

Maneuver fifty-gallon drums against some school doors or at work. Fill them with water. When the doors are opened, water spills out like a tidal wave.

Carry barrels onto the school rooftop or church building. Have beer slogans painted on the sides; from a distance they will look like giant beer cans. Then pour sand into them so that they can't be moved.

Bathrooms

When someone goes into the bathroom and locks the door, wait until he gets settled. Then secure the door so he can't come rushing out. Pour ammonia under the door. The smell usually overcomes the person, and he bangs on the door to get out. If you are really a cruel person, toss a firecracker into the bathroom.

Don't forget bathrooms are a good place for phone numbers. If you have grudges against old girlfriends, that's the place to write the numbers. It's fun to collect the numbers and have the guys bet on which one is a winner.

Beds

One of the old-time classics is to short-sheet a bed. When the person goes to bed, the sheet is so short it only comes up to his waist. When a person is very tired, this is frustrating.

Pour salt or some other granular substance onto the sheets to make the bed very uncomfortable to sleep in. The victim will try to brush the grains off, but, no matter how hard he tries, they remain. It is very disgusting. Another hard item to remove is toothbrush bristles. Cut the bristles off of several toothbrushes and spread them upon the bed sheet. Just try sweeping them out with your hand; they bounce all over.

A more grotesque item to place in a bed is animal guts. While I was at a buddy's house, his cat caught several rabbits and massacred them. I gathered up the parts and sealed them in clean plastic bags. His sister and I concealed the guts in his bed and dresser. When the victim came home drunk and got into bed, he nearly fainted. You can do the same with dead mice or other animals.

When a friend left on his honeymoon, several of our gang forced a way into his house and started our devious deeds. We took the box-spring mattress apart and hung several bells on the springs. Then we replaced the seams so that no one could tell we did anything to it. When the couple returned and became active in bed, they heard hundreds of ding-a-linging bells. Just the slightest movement causes them to ring; it is very disturbing to the lovers.

Some people tear all the labels off of canned goods, but I prefer to switch labels so the honeymooners don't know what they are choosing to eat. We usually hide the labels under the bed sheets to make it uncomfortable.

Beer

Neer-beer is a non-alcoholic beer, but it tastes the same; you can't tell the difference. When a few of us guys got together to drink, we invited a stooge. We gave the neer-beer to the stooge, and we drank the regular type. It was funny to watch the victim actually start acting drunk. There was no way in the world he could have gotten a buzz. It was all psychological. We got the biggest kick watching a person get drunk from no alcohol.

When we encountered a person who said it took twenty glasses of beer to get him drunk, we challenged him. However, I filled a quarter of the glass with vodka and the rest with beer. After two glasses, the guy was drunk and stumbling all over the room.

Blanks

If you are a firearms enthusiast, you may enjoy this one. I had Carl come out to the farm to do some target shooting. I supplied the pistols and ammo. I started off shooting and hitting the target. It was Carl's turn to shoot; he fired and fired but never hit the target. In the meantime, I was loading my gun with blanks to let him use next. He tried my gun but still didn't hit the target: however, every time I fired, I hit the target. This went on for a while, and I could tell he was getting disgusted. Finally I told Carl to check the target. when he got next to it, I pointed and began shooting. He almost fainted from fright while screaming at the same time. I laughed so hard I fell, and, as Carl cautiously made his way towards me, I explained. He was still in shock, so he couldn't appreciate it as much as I.

Tell your wife or friend you want her or him to see the new pistol you've just bought. Tell the person to dry-fire it to get the feel of it. (Dry-firing is the pulling of the trigger with no bullets in it.) Claim that it is not loaded and that there is nothing to fear. Secretly slip a blank cartridge into the cylinder. While the person is pulling the trigger he is relaxed, but when he gets the blank, and it explodes–look out! The poor victim will nearly have a heart attack. You can even act like you've been shot, and that will terrify everyone. A note of caution: don't let the pistol be pointed at anyone's face or at close range, because powder will still come from the cartridge and an injury may result.

Blind Dates

When it came to double-dating, if I could set a friend up with a girl I did my best to make it exciting. For example, once I set up a friend with a midget. At other times, it was usually a person of a different race. But surprisingly enough, the evenings usually turned out magnificently. But my friend's expression at first was usually worth a million dollars.

Blocks

With the autos getting smaller, this prank gets easier everyday. Lift up the rear of the car and place a block under the axle so that the tires are off the ground. When the person tries to drive away, he doesn't go anywhere because the tires are off the pavement. If you are really mean, attach a chain from the axle to a telephone pole. When he tries to pull away, he gets stopped–fast!

Brakes

In most cars, the brake light will come on when you depress the emergency brake pedal. However, depressing the pedal just a little will cause the light to come on without the brake's taking hold. If the brake light comes on while you are driving, it usually means you've lost your brakes and can't stop. The first time I tried this, I had two girls in the car with me. While driving down the highway, I secretly put pressure on the emergency brake until the light came on. Then I yelled, "Oh my gosh, I don't have any brakes!" When the girls saw the light, they got excited and started screaming. I told them to jump into the back seat and brace themselves for a collision. I also told them they better tell me how much they love me and what they would do for me. They made promises of love, because they thought they were goners. Well, I maneuvered the car off the highway, stopped, opened the hood, and made a bang or two. I got back in the car and told them I'd repair the brakes. Before I turned the ignition back on, I released the emergency brake so the light wouldn't show. Later I made the girls fulfill their promises. This practical joke is really a lot of fun, especially the reactions of people in the car with you and especially when going down a steep hill. Before you actually try this, experiment by yourself so you know how much pressure to apply.

Boogers

It's very unsightly to see someone pick his or her nose. You can bend your finger in half and position it at your nostril opening. this will look like your finger is about two inches up your nose. Or, while in a study hall or class, conceal a little wad of paper (I like to use Play doh best) in your hand so that when pretending to be digging for a booger, this wad falls onto the table. It will look like a booger and make others sick. Then you can flick it with your finger at someone and watch everyone scatter. Make some grunting sound while your finger is at your nose for distraction.

While playing with your nose, secretly take a broken rubber band up to your nostril. Hold one end up to your nose and stretch the other end. It will look like a long, slimy booger is coming and gross everyone out. Throw the

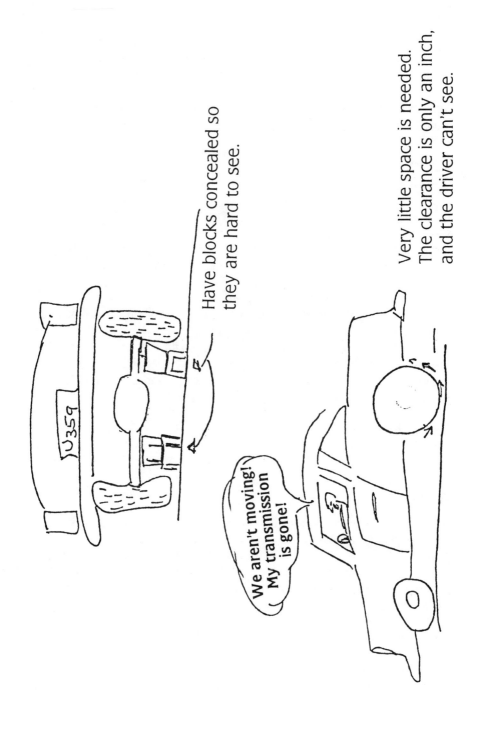

Make lots of noise to attract attention.

rubber band at people watching you, and they'll scream. And the victim will be the one getting into trouble at school for causing a loud disturbance.

Also, you can stick your index finger to your nostril and put your pinky finger to your lips to moisten it, then take your hand away and touch someone watching you with the wet finger. It's pretty convincing.

Just before you pretend to blow your nose in class or study hall or at a restaurant, secretly place some of the commercial Green Slime on your hanky. Take it to your nose and pretend to blow. While making the distracting noises, allow the Green Slime to ooze from the hanky onto the table. Sometimes people will get sick or leave the room.

Bumper Stickers

A Baptist church consulted me with a problem of theirs. The Methodist church next door to them was using their parking lot on Sunday mornings, leaving no space for the Baptist parishioners. I simply told them (for a small fee) to put, "I am Proud to be a Baptist" bumper stickers on all non-member cars in their lot. It wasn't long until the Methodist stopped parking off-limits. there was one stubborn fellow who still insisted on parking in the Baptist lot. We made a special sticker for him with reference to a Satanic church–he finally got the idea.

You can go to any novelty shop and have bumper stickers made for your particular practical joke.

Cake

Take an ordinary sponge and cover it with cake frosting. For a birthday or just for dessert, serve your decorated cake. When the hungry guest tries to cut the cake, he has all kinds of problems. He'll try and try and won't be able to cut it, and he won't be able to figure out why.

Surprise your birthday friend with a breast cake, and it'll leave him speechless. The boob cake *has* become popular, but there are some who haven't encountered it and are easily embarrassed. I send a friend down to the bakery to order a penis cake. He got laughed out of the store. However, there are a few places that make this cake. I advise you to call on the phone first to avoid embarrassment.

One of my favorite cake tricks deals with the trick candles. These commercial candles cannot be blown out. The birthday boy will huff and puff until he collapses, and the candles will still be on fire. No one will suspect foul play; people will think the guy is a weakling.

If you are really devious, dip some firecrackers in wax to masquerade as candles. Substitute the firecrackers for the candles and get out of sight. When the "candles" explode, cake flies everywhere and on everyone–what a mess!

Cancellations

Everyone has a special class at school he or she wishes to avoid occasionally. Some schools have cancellation slips; if yours does, swipe them. If not, have your own printed. I printed cancellation slips and posted them about thirty minutes before class began. The students would see it and just leave. The instructor would see the note and look dumbfounded.

If it is snowing and you don't feel like going to school, try this deed. Wake up early in the morning and call your local radio station. Say that you are the superintendent of schools and that you have canceled school because of bad weather, heating problems, etc. If the weather is warm, call the radio station to announce that school is canceled because of broken water pipes.

When honeymooners are on their way to their hotel, call ahead and cancel their reservation. They get to their destination and find out there is no place to stay. I have even canceled dinner reservations for people. The girl gets so angry with her boyfriend that she just about leaves him. She will think he is so stupid that he forgot to make the reservations.

This cancellation idea just may be the most important one to your sports career. I had a championship volleyball game with the fiercest team in our school. I had my special girlfriend anonymously call most of the male players on the other team, asking each one to meet her at a different location for romance. She told each one how great she thought he was that she had always wanted to meet him, and how great a lover she was and that it was the only chance she had to make love with him. The fellows' sexual appetites were greater than that for sports, and they each traveled to meet their secret admirer. The fellows got to the meeting place, and, naturally, no one was there. By the time they got to the game, it was over, and we had won by forfeit.

When the girl calls the fellows, be sure to get her to sound hot and sexy. Say that she should ask them to meet her at an out of the way spot, and tell her not to reveal herself. The journey has to take enough time that the players won't be able to get back to the game in time to play. It is even more embarrassing to send the boys to a motel room. They will knock on the door number the girl gave to them, and of course whoever is occupying the room will think he is nuts. This stunt really works. I tried it several times on many occasions. You see, the male is usually oversexed and doesn't think correctly when aroused. This doesn't work for females, because they have more common sense regarding sex.

When someone is absent from school or work, and people ask you if you know anything about it, just make up a ridiculous story. Tell people he was kidnapped or fired. The story soon spreads, and everyone feels foolish when the absentee person returns the next day.

Cast

I always wanted to gain some sympathy for a broken arm, so I had my friend, Ron, a nurse, get cast material and wrap my left arm. Presto: instant broken arm! I went to pick up my girlfriend for a Friday night date, and she was very shocked to see my injury. I told her I'd been stricken by a moving car and was lucky to be alive. I received the royal treatment from her at dinner and at the movies and especially when we went parking. When I dropped her off at 2:30 A.M., she woke her parents to tell them of my terrible ordeal, and I went home to saw off my cast. However, when I picked up her and her family on Sunday with no cast, their reaction was hilarious. I have also worn the cast and told people I was going to a faith healer. The next day, when they saw I'd been healed, the people were compelled to attend church. Anyone wishing to perform this prank can obtain the cast-wrap supplies from a medical supply outlet. Have your friend do a healing job on you and remove the cast. He is an instant celebrity.

Catsup

School lunches were usually boring, so to spice up the hour we unscrewed the catsup bottle lid. When the victim tried to pour some on his hot dog or hamburger, the entire contents of the bottle dumped onto the plate, making a big mess of the entire meal. We would just about fall off our chairs when a teacher got D.D. (Devious Dennised). I used this in college and public cafeterias to get a laugh while someone got embarrassed.

The first time I saw someone drink a bottle of catsup in a restaurant, I nearly got sick with the other customers. After a little practice, you acquire the taste and drink it down like a soft drink. Go in, order a bottle of catsup or drink the bottle on the table, and watch the people get sick.

The next time you have a picnic or any special occasion, have some phony squirt bottles of catsup. Have them sitting next to the real containers. Pick up the container and spurt your friends. A red string shoots out, looking like catsup, and scares the victim.

Whenever I have small children around, I act like I am slicing something with a knife and do my act: scream suddenly, hold your hand, and run frantically. Spread some catsup all over your hand to make it look serious. The little kids will think you are bleeding to death, and they'll be so scared that they'll wet their pants.

Cavities

There are special discoloration tablets that when chewed make the teeth turn an ugly color. If a person has a cavity, any type of tooth decay, or even if he didn't brush his teeth, this will show up. I used to say to friends, "Want some candy or a breath mint?" Then the fun begins, because it makes their teeth look terrible. Just talking embarrasses them! I used to grind them up in food to conceal what I had done. The results were the same. I did this to my girlfriend one night before she had a class at a night college. I fixed her dinner and ground up the tablets in her food. The poor girl was so nervous that she almost fainted. Yes, we split up for a week. But it wears off the teeth in about an hour. And if someone talks to you or asks questions, how can you keep from showing your teeth?

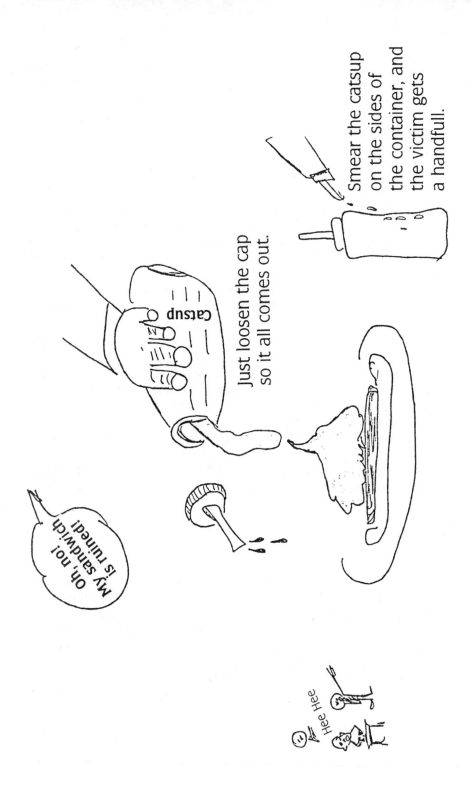

Celebrity

This charade works best if you have more people in on it. If you are in a restaurant or on a plane, make like some ordinary person is a famous person, either a sports star or an actor. Sit close to a stranger and talk to your accomplice about how great it would be to have that fellow's autograph. Usually the stooge will go up to that person for his signature and nearly die of embarrassment when he finds out the star is really a nobody.

Another set-up that involves an accomplice is the old shoe-size joke. Tell a person that Joe's father has large feet, that he wears size 16 shoes and really gets embarrassed if anyone talks about it. Convince your stooge to go ask Joe Blow about his father's shoe size to put him down. What your stooge doesn't know is that Joe is in on this practical joke, and the dialogue goes something like this:

Stooge: "Hey Joe, heard your dad really has large feet.
What size shoe does he wear, ha ha–elephant shoes?"
Joe: "It's really not funny. My dad got his legs cut off in a
car and train accident."
Stooge: "Oh, hey man, I am really sorry. I didn't know."

The stooge really feels lousy. How could he have said such a cruel thing? About five minutes later, you and Joe go up to him and tell him it was all a joke, that Joe's dad is fine. Once we had a girl start crying because she was so upset. This is a good time-killer while on lunch break.

Chairs

If you have an old chair you can sabotage, cut the legs so that when someone sits down it collapses, and the person rolls to the floor. The victim will think it is time to go on a diet. (Do *not* do this to an older person, because their bones are brittle.) Or, cut the seat so that when a person sits down his rear end heads for the floor, and gets stuck.

I used to carry a small container of water to classes. I would pour the water on the seat either before class or when the victim left his seat. The person usually sat down without looking and got a very wet bottom. It looks like he didn't get to the restroom in time.

Limburger Cheese

As you know, this is a very smelly item that can be used in a variety of ways. If you have a grudge against a car owner, put some limburger cheese on the manifold of the car engine. As the engine gets hot, the cheese melts and really stinks. Then the stink won't go away, because the cheese can't be removed. You can also put it in the tailpipe if it's easier.

Once I got angry at an adversary and bought ten pounds of limburger cheese. That night we smeared the cheese all over the sides of a house and on the gutters and spouting. We broke up chunks and threw them onto the roof. When the day got hot, the house really stunk. The cheese was baked into the roof and crevices. We saw the whole family trying to wash down the house.

So, if you want to stink something up, smear the cheese on anything. You can put it in the air ducts at school or in the corner of the classroom. But remember, wear gloves or keep the cheese in a container so that the smell doesn't get on your hands. In the locker room, smear the cheese on a guy's shoes, and when he goes to his next class everyone will move away from him.

Chickens

Live, loose chickens are the hardest thing to catch. I helped some county high school kids obtain one hundred chickens from the area poultry farmer. Then, during the night, we entered the school and let the birds loose. What a mess! It took the teachers a week to catch all the birds. There was chicken crap on the desks, floors, everywhere. Every time a teacher would go after a chicken, it would fly over the lights.

You don't have to live in the country to do this. If you've got the bucks, the farmer will sell.

The next time you invite someone over for dinner, serve a covered dish. When he or she takes the lid off of the dish, there lies a rubber chicken. You can fling a rubber chicken across the room or chase little children with it. It can be used for many purposes.

Cigarette Loads

If you can find commercial cigarette loads, you can have an exciting evening of watching explosions and startled smokers. There are also snow tablets that fill the room like a snowstorm. Now if you have none of the above, break off five match heads and stick them halfway down the victim's cigarette. As you dig out the tobacco, be sure not to tear or puncture the paper. When packing it back in, do a neat job. Finally, when the fire reaches the match heads, a flash of fire from the cigarette will light up the whole room.

There is a chemical called menthol blue that turns anything blue. You can sprinkle some in a cigarette and watch the victim's teeth turn blue as he inhales the smoke. This chemical can be obtained through your druggist or biology teacher. The stain remains for some time, so the victim will avoid any conversation.

Break off the match heads.

Four or five will give sufficient explosion.

And ready for the victim!

Carefully dig out the tobacco without tearing paper.

Match heads in place,

Tobacco packed back unnoticed,

Clerks

Whenever I am in Penneys or Sears, I head for the clothing department. I put on a sportcoat and tie and act like a sales clerk. It is great to have another person or two with you and explain that they are trainees. I go up to a customer and ask if he or she needs help. When the person asks about size or cost or anything, I give a terrible reply. "That load of coats was infested by rats in our back room, but we think we killed them all." Or, "No, we don't have fat people's clothes; you'll have to go to the tentmakers." It's hilarious to watch their expressions. If you have the nerve to try it in the women's underwear department, your comments are unlimited.

Coal

A lot of people burn coal to help heat their homes. The homeowner usually just calls the coal company, and a big truck just dumps the load in the yard. Well, you can call the company, order two or three tons of coal, and tell them to dump it in the front yard of the address you give. Then when the victim comes home and finds all this coal all over his yard he nearly faints. what can he do? He can't get the company to take it back. He has to pay and clean it up. This also works with a giant load of gravel. Have them dump it right in the middle of the driveway; this really makes it worse. If need be, you can wait at the house to sign the bill, with no one home who knows if you live there or not. However, I like just making the phone calls and leaving it at that.

Cockroaches

When you go into a restaurant, take a dead cockroach with you. If you don't have any cockroaches, any ugly bug will do. Keep the roach concealed until you are nearly done with your meal. Then, place it in your food. After it's in your food yell, "There's a bug in my food!" This will cause the manager to come running and he'll do anything to keep you quiet. It will result in a free meal just to keep you quiet. He doesn't want to lose any customers.

While we're discussing free meals, just get a friend to help you out. Sit at a dining counter and order just a cup of coffee. Have your friend come in and sit beside you but act like strangers. Let him order a big meal and finish it. Quickly switch bills and let him pay for the small tab. When you go to the register to pay the bill, exclaim that there must be some mistake, you only had coffee, etc. In the meantime, your friend has already gone, so no adjustment can be made. They only charge you for the coffee, and your buddy gets a free meal. The next time switch roles so that *you* get a free meal. This saves quite a bit of money on a trip.

Corn

I have talked to many kids now growing up who have never thrown corn on Halloween. For those of you who haven't, shell several ears of field corn into a sack. When it's dark, run from house to house and throw corn at the windows. Naturally, it startles the people inside, because it sounds like rocks hitting the windows. But why wait until October to do this? Do it year-round and catch everyone off-guard.

Cups

There are commercial dribble glasses; when a person is drinking, the cup causes liquid to dribble out and make a mess. You can't carry this dribble glass everywhere, or people will get suspicious. If someone is drinking from a plastic cup, poke a small hole just above the liquid level. When the person tips the cup to drink, liquid dribbles out onto him. Ask the victim to go get you something or drop something and ask him to pick it up. When he bends over, quickly poke a hole in the cup. This works well with milk cartons at school or in a cafeteria. Practice this on a cup at home so you'll know exactly where to poke the hole.

Cupboards

The next time you can be alone in a friend's kitchen, do some mischief. Arrange everything in the cupboards so that when they open up the doors everything falls out. It's not original, but effective.

I would always get my friend's wife in a frenzy when I would rearrange the contents of their cupboards. I would move the dishes to the canned goods section and totally confuse them. You need to be fast, but it can be accomplished in a minute. My sister had to go to the grocery three times before she found her misplaced food. She is currently undergoing counseling.

Greeting Cards

I have already discussed the sending of Mother's Day cards to the boss or to "friends" and, when a birth announcement appears in the newspaper the sending of a card with a different race to the family (and signing some else's name). The family gets a little annoyed when the picture on the card doesn't match their race. When Christmas time comes, some people enclose a little story of what the family has been doing. Pick a family and make up some outlandish story, like little Johnny was arrested for throwing eggs at the neighbors or little Debbie is pregnant and doesn't know who the father is. When word reaches this family of the bogus cards, they'll have a lot of explaining to do. These "fake" misspelled newsletters should be typed.

D

Doorbells

Nearly everyone has rung doorbells and then run. The victim comes to the door, and no one is there. When you do this several times to the same person, he gets very disgusted. I also like to add a variation to the prank. Take the homeowner's garden hose and stick it in his screen door. Then ring his doorbell, run to the nozzle, and turn on the water. When the victim opens the door, he gets soaking wet, and water goes everywhere.

Desk

While sitting at a desk in class or study hall, one can get a lot of attention by acting sleepy. Have one arm holding your head, but make it wobble as if you keep dozing. Keep your other arm underneath the table. Because you are slightly bent over, the other arm can freely extend under the table. Let your head start to fall towards the table but bring it back. By now you will have several people watching you and waiting for you to do something silly. Finally, let your head fall toward the desk top, but just before it hits, stop! Raise your arm under the table up against the underneath so that there is a loud knock. Everyone will think you really hit your head and they will scream. Actually, your head falls fast enough for your hair to touch the desk top so that no one can tell any difference. Let your head look like it is bouncing off the table, and then lay it flat. The girls will think you are knocked out, and you'll get pampered.

When sitting at a long desk in study hall across from a girl, I would make her scream and embarrass herself. Most girls sit with their legs spread apart because they don't think anyone can see under the table. Take your shoe off and stick your foot between her legs, right into her crotch. She'll jump a little and giggle, and everyone will look at her. She will be too embarrassed

Ring the door bell several times. After the third time, position the garden hose in the screen door. When the angry homeowner comes rushing to the door, turn on the garden hose and he gets soaking wet.

to tell what you did. Remember to take your shoe off so as not to get her panties dirty and leave evidence in case she does tell the teacher. Taking your shoe off allows your foot to slide between her legs more easily.

This trick is really fun to pull on co-workers and even more so on a teacher who has just left the room. Pull a drawer out and put a ruler across the top so the books and contents don't fall out when you turn it upside down and replace it. The teacher comes back and opens the drawer, and books come crashing to the floor. He or she will be mad enough to kill, so don't get caught.

Dummies

We used to get a big kick out of making a lifelike dummy and waiting for a passing motorist. We would toss the dummy in front of the car (from a camouflaged area) and hear the tires come to a squealing halt and worried people running out of their cars, thinking they ran over a pedestrian.

If you are innovative, string a wire above the road and pull the dummy across with it. It will look like the dummy is running across the road; in reality, you are pulling it. Give a yell of pain: it's more convincing.

Hang the dummy from a telephone pole or tree on any public street and watch the reactions of people going by. Be careful not to hurt anyone.

Ditto

This is a special kind of paper that makes several copies for class handouts or anything. There is usually a paper between the blue impressionable copy and the outside copy with the writing. Every chance I got, I would slip out the protective copy, take my fingernail, and write a swear word in a few special places. It can't be seen on the outside cover, but, when it is printed, the words appear. If the teacher doesn't catch it, it goes to the students.

Ask to proofread a friend's paper before he hands it in then write in some extra words, like how much the instructor stinks, how ugly he is, etc. The student won't know anything is wrong until the instructor calls him in for conference. I tried to make a few friends laugh by doing this on my own paper; however I forgot to erase it before I handed it in.

Borrow a textbook for a few seconds and write some obscenities on the outside pages between the hard cover. The person usually doesn't discover it for several days, but everyone else does.

Take an inflatable female dummy and tape it to a friend's car at work, advertising 1-800-DOL LOVE.

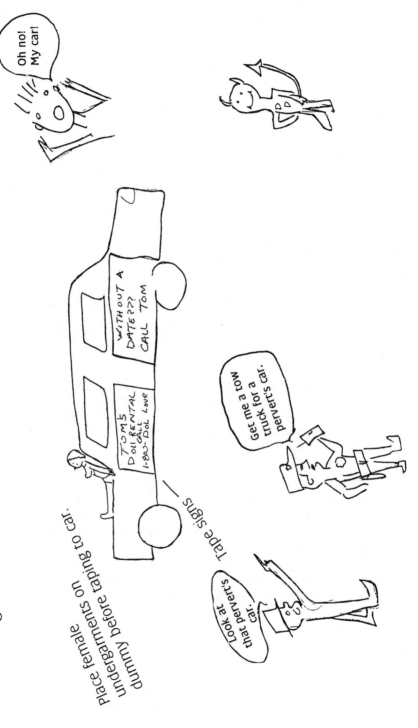

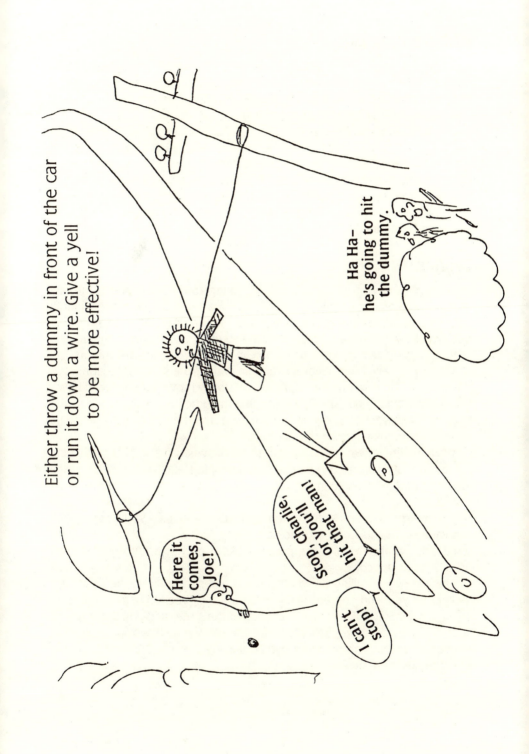

Dishwashing Liquid

It is funny to watch the reaction of the victim when he grabs his car door handle, makes a face, and acts like he grabbed a hand full of manure. At a fraternity meeting, we watched Brother Bob squirm when he grabbed his car door handle. He wiped it, but it didn't come off. Finally, about two weeks later, Bob telephoned me and said, "Hey Dennis, I finally got your joke off my car. It started to rain, and the handles bubbled up and got clean." That's all it takes–water to clean it. It is especially funny to watch a teacher grab a classroom door and get a messy hand. We were standing outside a bar one night when a drunk grabbed the handle and slipped. We told him some fellow had just ejaculated on it, and the drunk got sick and vomited. I've always preferred IVORY liquid.

Driving

Anytime you drive and try a prank, it's dangerous. These pranks usually require some practice. While driving down a road, you can sit in the window with your hands on the roof and look like you are steering with your feet, but actually you have a buddy doing the steering way down in the driver's seat. You just give him directions. You can do this yourself with mirrors.

When you have three fellows sitting up in the front seat, try to sit next to the window. Then when at a stoplight or in slowly moving traffic, bend down like you are tying your shoes. It looks like the other two fellows are sitting together like lovers. I usually end up laughing, and they try to get me up. It's really embarrassing for the macho male.

While driving down the road, put on a Halloween mask. This really gets some stares and surprised looks from other people. I like to wear them around July. Any month other than October is good because the people just don't expect it.

If there are children parked in the car next to you, pres your face against the window. This distorts the face and looks funny. Or, just stick out your tongue and make faces. If the parent looks over, just act normal; the kid usually gets slapped.

I always enjoy pulling up to a small kid and saying, "Hey, the police are looking for you, and you are really in big trouble." The kid usually takes off crying for home. Or, if you are driving down the street and you see a friend, start honking your horn; he'll recognize the car and start waving. But wave to the opposite side of the street instead. If a guy is with a girlfriend, it usually embarrasses them both.

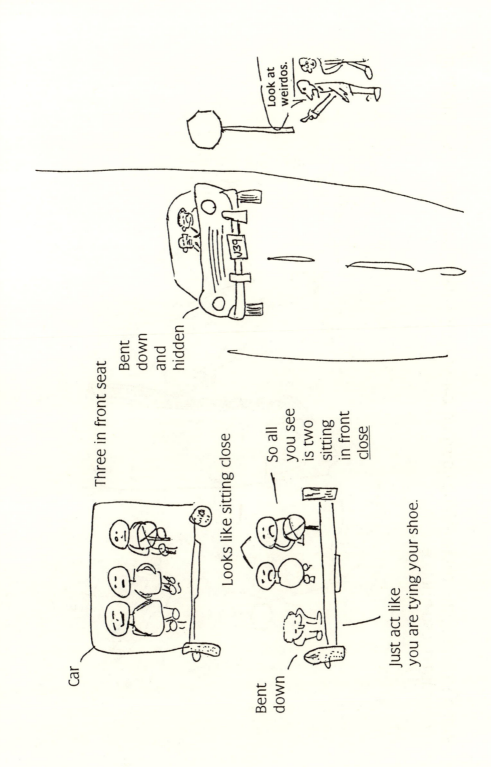

When smearing the dishwashing liquid on car or door handles, do it thinly enough that the victim doesn't notice.

Dogfood

The next time you have guests over for lunch, scare them with your shocking food. Have ham salad mixed up ahead of time to serve on the plates. Have Kal Can on the counter, dig it out onto the plate, and set it in front of your guests. In reality, you have ham salad on your plate, start gulping it down. Growl and bark while chewing it. The guests will think you are eating dogfood and just refuse to eat.

The Kal Can dogfood resembles dog excrement. Dump piles of the dogfood on the steps. When people come down the steps (especially in their bare feet) and step in the dogfood, they think they have stepped in dog poop. Oh, what a terrible feeling, when it goes between your toes! At home, school, the pool or anywhere this prank has its effect.

Doorways

When I spent time in dorms, I would wait for everyone to go to sleep and then brick up doorways of various rooms. When the person woke up and opened his door to leave, he found it bricked up and thought he was sealed in. The only way he could get out was to knock the wall down. Sometimes I liked to use mortar when bricking up a doorway of someone who really deserved it. This makes it more difficult to get out of the room or house.

Usually in the back of stores there are metal cartons stacked up for the delivery people to retrieve. Stack the cartons at the back exit in front of the doorway. Create a disturbance or yell that you're a delivery man. When the store employee opens the door, the cartons all come crashing and make a terribly loud noise.

Even though this prank is old and nothing spectacular, it is still funny, and I like to use it. Position a bucket of water over a doorway so that the next person who opens the door gets wet. In order for this to work, don't close the door but leave it open just enough for the container to rest comfortably. You can place water balloons over the door for the same effect or just some magazines.

Some people are extremely scared of spiders and snakes, even rubber ones. Place several plastic spiders or a snake above the doorway so that when the door is opened, the person has a spider fall on his shoulder.

The age-old bucket over the doorway never fails.

OR

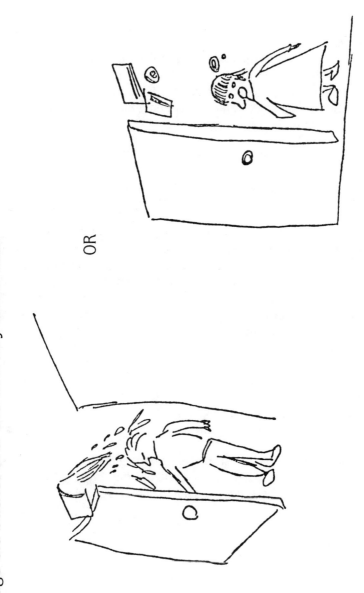

If you don't want a wet mess, place magazines and booklets above the doorway. It's less messy, and no one gets hurt.

Fill your friend's hat with water at work or school.

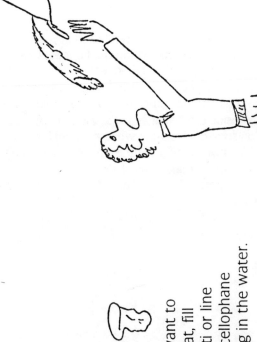

Make sure it's upside down.

If you don't want to ruin a good hat, fill it with confetti or line the hat with cellophane before pouring in the water.

Deodorant

If you're like me, you get tired of everyone's borrowing your deodorant in the locker room. By the time everyone else gets done with it, there is none left. So I took a small can of spraypaint, made a label that looked like a brand-name deodorant and took it with me to the locker room. I said, "Someone left his deodorant–here wanna use it?" The first guy who sprayed it under his arm got black paint in his pit. It was really hilarious.

Remember to conceal the paint label and do a professional job on the fake label. It will be well worth the time. In the locker room, act like you found it. This may save you from a broken nose. You could give it to your coach as a present and sign someone else's name to it.

Diaper

There is a dirty diaper joke I purchased that really gets results. Just try leaving this dirty diaper in a restaurant or on the floor at school. It is so real-looking that people don't want to get near it.

The easiest way to get diapers is to buy the disposable ones in the grocery store. While you're there, purchase some peanut butter. Just smear the peanut butter inside the diaper, and it's instant baby crap. I enjoy placing the dirty diaper on someone's seat at work, a school function, or car just to gross people out. Then I would offer to take it away, slip my fingers into the "mess," and lick them. It really makes the stooge sick.

If you are too embarrassed to buy diapers, just drop me a note and I'll help you out.

E

Eggs

One of my favorite tricks at Easter is to color my eggs without hard-boiling any. Then I secretly place them in my relatives' baskets, and the kids sure made a mess when they get home. I used to make elaborate baskets of junk and rotten food and put them in city hall with a sign: Free From the Mayor.

Take a dozen eggs, make a pinhole in the bottom, and drain all the filling. Place the eggs back in the carton and walk toward a sitting relative while exclaiming how great these eggs are. Accidentally trip, flinging the empty eggs at the person, and watch the victim jump. I had an aunt wet her pants over this.

If you have a grudge against a grocery store, hard-boil some eggs and substitute them for his good eggs.

Entrance

When you are going into an establishment with a friend, open the door and let him go in first, then yell out, "Where's the toilet?" Then step back and shut the door so that only your friend is seen. Everyone thinks your friend screamed when you it was really you, but, because you are outside behind the door, no one sees you. This really makes the person on the inside look foolish. It's a good way to dump a girlfriend you don't want anymore.

A similar trick can be used when a person is getting ready to leave an establishment. You leave about ten seconds ahead of time and then jam the door with your foot so that he can't open the door. Then make weird noises and talk in high pitched tones: "I can't get out, darn, darn, darn." This action makes it sound like the person trying to get out is making the weird noises. It's very embarrassing for the victim. Remember: it only works on a door that people can't see through.

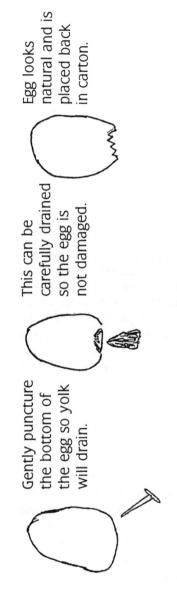

Do your fake trip and let your eggs fall toward your victim–and listen for the screams!

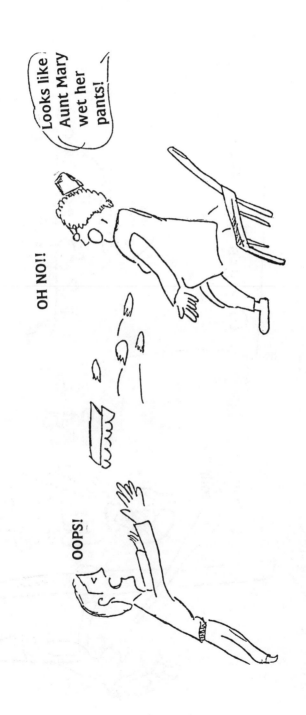

Let your friend go inside an establishment first. Then quickly step back OUTSIDE so you can't be seen. Just as you are stepping back out, yell, "Here I am, everyone," or "Where's your toilet?" The only person seen near the door is your friend, and does he ever get embarrassed!

(It is a good way to get rid of an unwanted girlfriend.)

Tell your friend to go to the door of an open classroom of girls. Tell him that a girl looks familiar and you want him to check it out.

As your victim is standing in the doorway in plain view, YOU stand back so not to be seen and say something embarrassing. Only your friend will be seen and look silly.

While in the classroom, library, or anywhere with your friend, walk out of the room ten seconds before he or she does. Then hold the door so it will not open as the victim tries to open it. Talk in a high-pitched voice and sound like a sissy. It will appear that the victim is the one talking, and it is very embarrassing.

Engagements

If you have a grudge against a girl or if she is the kind of girl who thinks she has all the answers to life or is a teaser, this is fabulous. Place her picture in the newspaper under Engagements to Marry. Invent a groom who is a garbage man or sewer worker with very embarrassing details. When we placed ours, we used the class mental bimbo. It was hilarious for several weeks. You can also write anonymous letters of congratulations to rub it in. One could include a picture of the groom and make it a person of a different race, creed, or color, just for laughs.

Engine Stunts

I never liked to have my car messed with, like most people, so if you get caught, expect a fight.

When they were available, I would attach "whistle bang bombs" to the spark plug of a car. As soon as the victim turns the key to start the engine, the whistle begins, followed by the explosion and smoke rolling from the car. A person really jumps from the car fast, not knowing what is going to happen next. Incidentally, this caused my fiancee to break our engagement, so be prudent in selection of victims.

Now, if you don't have the proper item, make your own. Take a firecracker and a smoke bomb and hook on a spark plug. Recap the rubber conductor over the plug. When the car is started, boom–the same effect.

Eye

Seventy percent of our population wear eyeglasses, so this dirty trick is easy. Ask to borrow a victims's glasses for a minute. While you have them in your possession, soap the lenses so he can't see.

Nearly everyone likes to look at nude pictures. You can buy one of those little scope containers with an interesting picture inside. While the person is looking, the container rests against the eye and blackens it. This black eye joke is totally unknown to the victim until he notices people staring at him.

F

Fire Extinguisher

When I would get bored, I would con my friends into helping me to "borrow" a fire extinguisher. I would climb into the trunk of our car and, when we stopped for a red light, open the trunk up and spray the car behind us. The fog catches the person in back by surprise. He doesn't know what to do. We sometimes would spray the extinguisher while driving down the road so that the car appears to be smoking. We chase each other down the middle of the road spraying each other. Laughter catches the other motorists by surprise.

Farts

If I know our gang is going to drive somewhere and be in close contact, I make sure that I eat plenty of beans, preferably soup beans. Then, while riding, I let out a juicy "silent but deadly" fart. Someone always asks, "Who died?" and they start rolling down the car windows. Trouble is, I would start laughing hysterically and give myself away. I would stink up the auto so bad the guys would pull off the road and jump out then get back in, and I start farting again. I also like to stand in a group, release a silent stinker, and move away. The aroma lingers, and the people can't figure out who stinks up the place. I do this moving fart in the supermarket all the time.

Ask your friend to try to find a spot or tear on the seat of your pants, and, then his or her face is close to your rump, cut a loud stinker.

When you are in bed with your girl or wife, tell her to get under the covers because you are going to spit. Once her head is under the covers, rip off a loud stinker.

When you and the gang are stopped at a traffic light or at a drive-around restaurant, have everyone jump out of the car and hold their noses. Wave your hands, and it'll look like the car stinks unbearably.

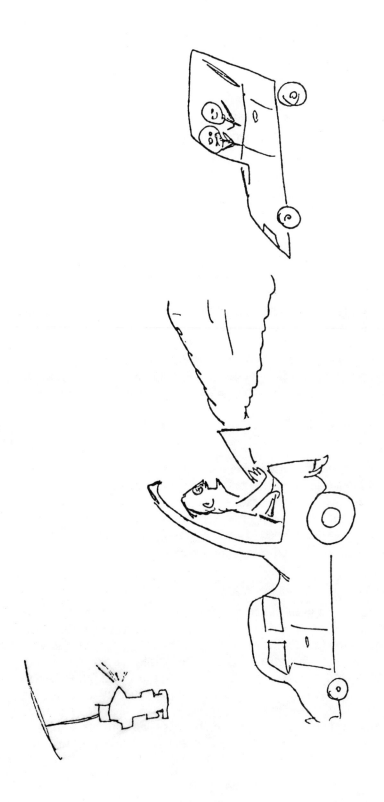

While stopped at a light, quickly pop open the trunk and spray the car behind with a CO_2 fire extinguisher.

Fake Fights

At school, if you want to trick the teacher, form a circle like the kids do when there is a fight, yelling for their favorite person to win. Instead of fighting, have the two fellows sit on the ground and play cards or a game. The teacher comes running up and is embarrassed to find he got all excited over nothing.

Flag Pole

Our gang used to run our insignia up the flag pole of the school and surprise the school officials. Make any type of picture or writing on an old sheet and run it up the flag pole. Then tie it in such a manner that it takes a while to get it down.

Take several pairs of old undershorts and run those up the flag pole. The school administration will really be embarrassed when everyone spies this disgusting sight.

I was contacted by some seniors for a prank to pull their last year in school. It was a country school, isolated from houses. I gave my expensive advice, and it came out just right. Rent a forklift or a corn elevator to put you at the top of the flag pole then take several old tires and slide them down the pole. In the morning, the people will not be able to tell how the tires got there. Also, the maintenance people won't be able to remove the tires for quite some time.

Fishing Line

Attach an old hat to some fishing line and hide about a block away. When someone attempts to pick up the hat, start reeling the line. Every time the fool attempts to pick up the hat, reel it in some more.

If you really want some fun, wad up a ten dollar bill and attach it to your line. People are more determined to get it. As many times as they bend down to pick it up, just reel a little more, keeping ahead of them.

Fireplaces

Naturally, smoke rises from the chimney unless it is obstructed. While the homeowner has a good fire going and the smoke is rolling out of the stack, quickly climb to the top and do your devious deed. Clog the opening with fiberglass, stereo foam, or even a plank of wood. This keeps the smoke from escaping and instead, causes it to back out and fill the whole house. Before the homeowner knows what's happening, it's too late. He'll try to put the fire out, but it will take time, because throwing water on the fire will temporarily cause it to smoke more. Soon the whole house is filled with black smoke—what a mess. Don't worry about getting chased or caught, because the

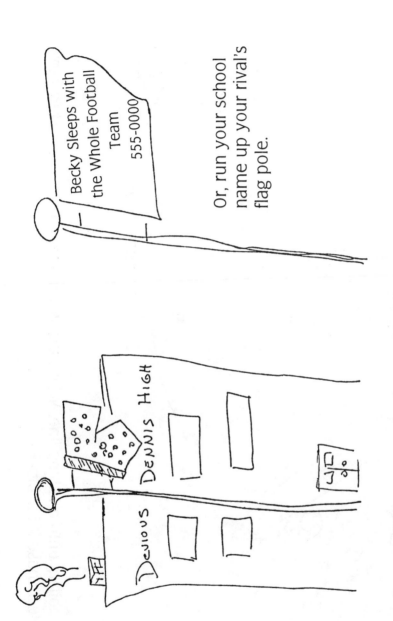

Or, run your school name up your rival's flag pole.

Run some underwear up your high school flag pole, then tie the rope so it's impossible to get down!

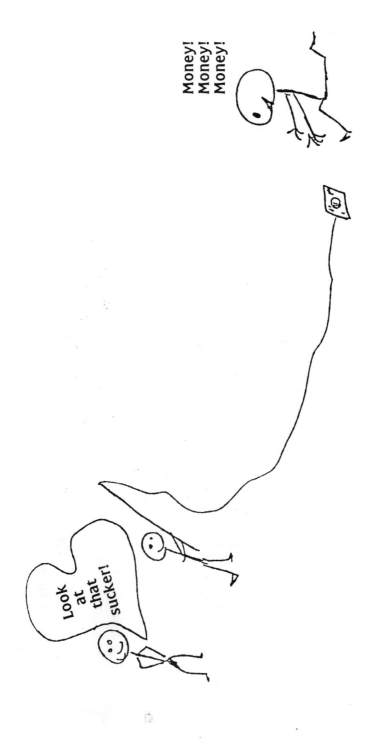

Hook ten dollars onto a fishing line. When the victim tries to pick it up, start reeling in the line. He'll chase it for blocks.

homeowner will be too concerned about checking his flue and trying to put the fire out rather than chasing someone.

Now, if you want to startle the homeowner fast, drop four water balloons down the chimney. The crash and sudden appearance of water will get the smoke rolling.

The soot that is in the fireplace is extremely messy and hard to clean. There is a Magic Soot on the market that resembles the black dust. I ordered this trick dust and took it to my sister's house. I scattered it on the floor, and she nearly fainted. It can be cleaned up very easily, but the sight of it is disgusting. I have used this several times at parties, and it usually causes mayhem.

Firecrackers

Take a firecracker and put the fuse halfway down in a lit cigarette. Then place it somewhere in the school restroom. This will give you enough time to get away so that, when it explodes, you are not suspected.

You can buy fake firecrackers and scare people by throwing them. I used to go to parties and pretend to be drunk, then place the fake firecracker in my mouth and light it. The people's expressions are sheer horror.

Put several cherry bombs down the commode, and they'll blow it off the bathroom floor. It just makes the day at school go faster.

Fits

A fit is quite an attention-getter, especially in a fast-food place, classroom, or any public area. Fall to the floor, kicking your legs and flopping your arms. Rotate your body on the floor while kicking chairs and howling with weird noises. This action really shocks people. This prank is useful to get you out of a test. have a couple of your friends escort you out of the room and then skedaddle. This can be used as a decoy in a restaurant for a free meal. Remember, no smiling, or your superior will realize it's a prank.

Fountains

Place some gum so it obstructs the water flow on a water fountain. When someone goes to get a drink, the water squirts out to the side and gets the drinker soaking wet. If you don't have gum, use tape or anything else to obstruct the water opening.

Some public places have water fountains that flow all night. I am talking about the kind with the water reservoir and the little statues. At night, take ten boxes of bubble bath (the more the better) and pour them into the fountain. There will be so many bubbles that people won't be able to get near the building. Mountains of bubbles and suds will be everywhere.

Filmstrips

This prank is almost impossible to do unless you have an AV friend. Cut out part of the film and splice it with part of a stag film. While the class is watching a history lesson, there suddenly appear nude girls and fellows in the midst of fun and games. What a shock to the teachers! This has to be planned very carefully and technically done.

I found this next joke much easier and have done it many more times. When the teacher is showing a demonstration using a slide projector, substitute a slide with some sexually explicit nude people. The teacher gets embarrassed, and the class has a good laugh. It is best too slip the slide in before class or during a break. I used to send for the nude slides from the popular skin magazines. The magazines have all types of ads, and these slides are easy to obtain. It is a lot of fun to do.

Now, if you don't have the above materials, the next best solution is a centerfold pinup. Tear the nude picture from the magazine and tape it to the screen to be used. The screen usually folds up, and no one knows there is a nude picture until the screen is pulled down. Then the fun begins as the unsuspecting teacher tries to hide the picture. This can be done long before class starts so that no one gets the blame.

G

Garage Sale

I placed ads in all area papers that there was an inside antique sale at a friend's house. The sale was to start at 6:00 A.M. I even placed signs down the road from the house. When they awoke, their driveway was filled with strangers; the children even let a few inside.

Gas

With gasoline being so expensive now, any temporary reduction in price brings in a crowd. To cause a gigantic line-up, motorists, just follow this little plan. After the station closes, paint a giant sign that says that for one day only (tomorrow), gas will be $.30 a gallon until sold out–open at 7:00 A.M. Cars will start linging up around 6:00 A.M., and, when the owner arrives, the line will be two miles long. When he tries to tell them it was all a hoax, a riot will break out, and all the excitement begins.

Some people brag about terrific gas mileage. I had a friend who thought he got 100 miles to a gallon of gas. Why? Because every night I emptied an extra gallon or two into his car without his knowledge. This went on for a while until I thought he acted too foolishly.

You have to be quick on this dirty trick so as not to be caught or set yourself on fire. In the middle of the street, quickly pour some gas on newspapers or cardboard and ignite. The motorists will have to wait until it goes out. It's interesting to watch the motorists' reactions.

I used to drive into a gas station with a horny broad then tell the attendant to fill 'er up. While the attendant was washing the windshield, I would start undressing the girl and "making it" with her. It's amazing how it can take ten minutes to clean the same spot on the windshield. Then I would tell the guy

I would give him the girl's phone number if he would let me have the gas free. The guy usually would; however, the number would just be a phone booth.

Gorilla

If you want to startle people in a bar, just put a guy in a rented gorilla suit and bring him in on a leash. First walk in and say you have a friend that can beat up anyone in the place. Get the fellow all riled up and watch them run out the back door. I like to run across an intersection packed with motorists and have the gorilla chase me. It's funny to have the gorilla jump on the hoods of the cars.

Glue

One of my favorite dirty tricks was to take glue with me to gym class. I'd wait till everyone left and then glue some of the guys' shoes to the floor. Don't do everyones or else the victim will be able to figure out who did it. It usually makes the person late for class, plus the janitor has to come with a wrecking bar to pry the shoes loose.

This also works in the classroom with someone's books. While sitting behind someone, lift the books and squirt the glue. A girl usually gets more embarrassed. This also works with briefcases at the office.

Also, try it on a quarter in the hallway. Some idiot will try all day to get it, only making a fool of himself.

Some glues are so effective that you can smear them all around a door, and then you just can't open it. This is one way to delay a school class. Class just may be canceled.

Glue the lid to any container so it won't open, even the inside lid of a mailbox. The victim will try all day before frustrated, he saws it open.

Once I glued my co-workers phone so it couldn't be answered; I also glued other items on his desk. He got so upset he had to be restrained by security. Lost that promotion, too.

Grapes

This prank is a real gross-out especially in a restaurant or school cafeteria. Skin a grape so that the glossy jelly part is showing. When you are done, it will look like mucous, a green hocker from your throat. Next, have it concealed in your hand and start pretending you are clearing your throat like you are bringing up a hocker. Bring your hand up to your mouth, act like you spit the grape in your hand, and show everyone. This really makes everyone nauseous. But you really send everyone running when you slurp the grape back up in your mouth and swallow it!

Golf

If you are a golfer, take some trick golf balls with you. Substitute a trick ball for your friend's ball. When he hits the ball, it will go just the opposite direction he hit it. There are also the ones that explode and split into a parachute.

We often would wait until a golfer's ball would roll up to a green and then toss our own extra balls onto the green. Usually he doesn't know which is his ball. We often would stuff the hole with manure, dog food, or limburger cheese. When the golfer has to reach into the hole to retrieve his ball, he nearly gags. This joke is also fun to do at the Putt Putt golf centers.

While taking a shortcut through the golf course with friends, I would take a ball out of my pocket and hit a friend easily with the ball. At the same time, I would call out that a golf ball was coming. I would pick up the ball, and we would all take off running while the friend thought he had actually been hit by a golfer.

Gifts

I have always enjoyed giving gifts at parties. However, when my gift is opened, it is quite a shocker. Take your own real gift but also smuggle a joke item. You can wrap up an old baby doll, Kotex, rubber, bra, or just some garbage. Let's say you are at a girl's party, she has opened all the gifts, and they have been traced to everyone. Then she opens the gift with no name tag and finds an old rubber. Surprise and embarrassment will be exhibited. If you really want to be nasty, put someone elses name on the package. That poor person will then be accused of giving the disgusting gift.

Remember not to let anyone see you bring in the fake gift and to act surprised along with everyone else to avoid suspicion.

Greetings

Go to a public area, where people are free to walk around. Be at one end of a walkway with a single person walking towards you. Have your partner about twenty feet behind the victim. As the victim is coming towards you, start saying, "How've you been? Good to see you." Wave your hands and have one extended. Naturally, the "man in the middle" thinks you are greeting him, and he smiles and extends his hand. But you just pass him and go to the person behind him and shake his hand. The victim runs to hide his embarrassment.

Most businesspeople have greeting cards to promote themselves. Even police officers carry cards so they can be contacted by witnesses. Once the professional person has his cards made, he rarely inspects them; he just passes them out to people he wishes to impress. Take one of the victim's

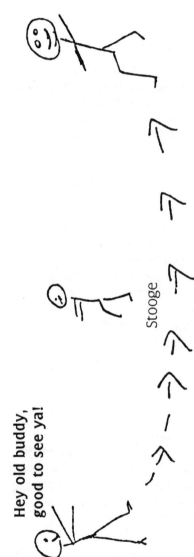

Hey old buddy, good to see ya!

Stooge

With your victim in the middle, act as if you are greeting him when it is really your friend behind him!

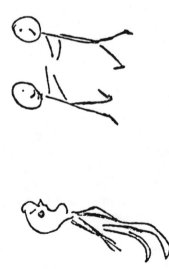

Your victim will be so embarrassed, he could die!

cards and model a zany one after it. Place your own words and his emblem in the same place so he can't detect jut by looking at it. Where it says "Patrolman Bob Smith," you substitute "Patrolman BM Steer" and change the other words. Just go to any print shop and they will make up what you want. Once you get the cards, secretly mingle them with the victim's so that he doesn't know they exist. When he hands out his trick card to a client, and the client looks flabbergasted, he'll be shocked to find out why. If you can't find a printer for this joke, I probably can, but it will be expensive.

This dirty trick really works a little easier when leaving. Cause a girl to have to get your attention in public. If the victim calls your name like she wants you for something, all the better. I try to leave behind a small object so she'll come running, calling my name. That's when you shout out a remark that will make her feel two feet tall. Victim: :Dennis, wait." Then shout in front of everyone, "No, Julie, I won't sleep with you and that's final!" Then hop in your car and take off. Everyone will look at her like she is some kind of tramp.

When I am introduced to a friend's girl, I usually say, "Oh, Bob has told me so much I could write a book. Do you have a sister as wild as you are? If you do, I would like to take her out."

When you are introduced to a buddy's girl, just say, "This isn't the one you were with last night; she has blonde hair."

Gum

Place chewed gum under a plate in a restaurant. The water is so hot in the dishwasher that it causes the gum to melt and get all over everything. It is nearly impossible to get everything clean.

I try to carry that novelty awful-tasting gum for rare occasions. Usually a kid will pester you for a piece of gum. When he starts chewing and it tastes so terrible, the victim almost chokes.

Also, "snap gum" is a way of getting rid of moochers. Inside the gum container is a mouse trap so that when the victim takes a piece, his finger gets smashed. This is a popular item in novelty catalogues.

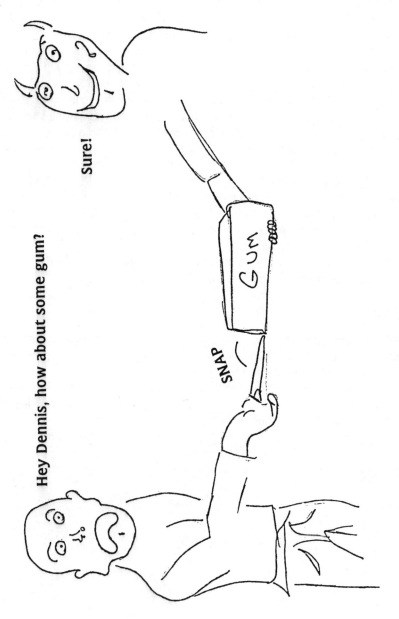

H

Hanging

Although this is extremely dangerous, it has its effects, even on the most cool-headed person. Tie the rope around your chest under your arms, NOT *around your neck!* Connect the part that goes around your neck only loosely so that no injury results. It's best to have a friend in on this; that way, if something goes wrong, he can help you out. This is really a shocker in the school bathroom. When a person comes into the bathroom and sees you, he'll go screaming for help. Then quickly come down. When people come to help, the victim will feel so foolish because there is nothing hanging there. Don't try this without assistance. Don't do any prank that would cause anyone to get hurt.

Hearing Aids

There was a fellow in our fraternity who wore a hearing aid, and when we would first approach him, we would move our lips to pretend we were talking. Well, he thought his hearing aid wasn't working, so he would turn the volume up all the way. Then we would shout at him. The loudness nearly knocked him off his feet. This works all the time, so try it on your nasty relatives.

Handcuffs

We really used to get the looks from people when we played detective in a restaurant. What you do is to have two fellows dressed up in sport coats, looking respectable. The third person is shabby-looking and in handcuffs. Walk into a restaurant and order some food. Have the fake criminal get mouthy and then slap him–this really startles the other customers. Have a loud dialogue about how he murdered someone, is a gangster, stole a car, etc. Talk loudly enough so that others can hear you. Handcuff the bad guy while you go to the restroom and let him eat with one hand. You'll be talking for days about how much fun it was.

Hitchhiking

I used to hitchhike everywhere I went. When there would be five of us, it would be hard to get a ride, so some would hide. The poor driver really got a surprise when he'd pull over to pick up one person and suddenly ten people started jumping into his car.

Or, if you are driving, pull over to pick up a hitchhiker. Just as he gets to the door, drive away. Do it over and over and the person gets disgusted and decides to walk.

Hair Dryers

Disassemble a hair dryer and wrap a wick of a firecracker around the hot coil. When the victim turns it on, the coils get hot in a matter of seconds, lighting the fuse. *Boom.* I always like to pull this in the locker room. Leave an abandoned hair dryer lying around; someone is bound to grab it.

Hair

Ask someone if he or she has ever seen a hair bleed. Usually the person says no, and you can proceed to demonstrate. Take a lone hair and place in a small amount of water. If you cup your hand, you can fill your palm. Say that just bending the hair makes it start it to bleed. You placed it in water so it can be seen more easily. Tell the person that he has to get really close to see it. When he does, smash the water with your other hand, and the water splashes the victim in the face.

Take a bald-head mask and place it over your head, covering your hair. Then, take a real wig and place on top of the bad cap. Attach a fine wire to the wig and run it down through your shirt. While eating a meal in a public area, sneeze or cough to attract the other people's attention. Then slowly pull on the wire so that the wig starts to slip off of your head. Other people start watching as your hair falls off and get a real surprise when there is a bald head where a hairy one was.

Remember if you grab someone's toupee or wig, you had better be faster or bigger or else you will get a black eye.

**Have you ever, ever seen a hair bleed?
You must look closely!**

Just as your victim gets his face to the water, throw your hand into the water, getting him wet!

Hands

Fake hands can scare an unsuspecting person just by being inside a closet door. But I get the most kicks out of having the fake hand hanging out of the trunk of my car. I get strange looks from other motorists. I even got pulled over by the police. They thought I had a corpse in the trunk.

There is a full-sized rubber hand with a stem you can buy. Stick the stem up your sleeve and hold it with your real hand. this fake hand looks so real that no one can notice until you shake hands. When the victim grabs your hand to shake, turn, leaving him holding your hand. It will really startle him and others.

I love to use the hand jolt buzzer. It is a wind-up gizmo that can be concealed in your hand. When you're shaking a victim's hand, it will give a tickling shock. I have also run wires from a battery down my arm into my hand. Have your hand insulated so you don't feel the electric. When a person grabs your special electrode hand, it knocks him off his feet. This takes quite a bit of electrical know-how, but it is worth it.

If you don't have any of these items, just smear some grease in the palm of your hand. When a victim shakes your hand, he'll feel something slimy. Tell him you just cleaned the commode.

Hankies

While in a quiet restaurant or class, blow your nose loud to create a disturbance. You can buy those special hankies, but I just like to cover my nose and stick out my tongue and blow. It really is loud, and no one can tell what you are doing. They just laugh because it's so loud.

Horns

Instead of pinning a horn at Halloween, it's more confusing to take a separate car horn, lay it underneath the car, and string the wire several feet away to where you can control the sound. Let the horn roar and just as the person comes out to the car, shut off the sound. When the person goes back inside the house, start it all over again. The victim will eventually disconnect his battery, but it won't stop the horn from blowing.

When someone steps in front of your car to check a tire or the hood or to open the garage door, blast the horn and he usually jumps three feet.

While riding down the highway with a friend, bend down so other motorists can't see you. Then reach up and start honking the horn. The other motorists will look at your car and stare. Pretty soon everyone on the highway will be looking at the driver. The driver will feel so foolish, because he is the only one the other people see. The driver can't stop you from honking the

This really works great on introductions.

Look at his face when he grabs your hand to shake and pulls it off your arm!

Honking the horn makes the driver look very foolish.

Bend down far enough not to be seen–it is more effective.

horn, because he could lose control and wreck. So he has to endure the embarrassment.

Some commercial places offer different, strange-sounding horns. My favorite is the horn that sounds like you are squealing your tires. When stopped at a cross-walk while someone is walking in front of your car, press on your horn. The squealing-tires sound makes the victim jump, because he thinks he is about to be run down.

Hold It

I used to enjoy going into a bar bathroom and standing at the urinal next to a drunk. I would grunt and groan and sigh, but I would actually have a sausage hanging out of my zipper, pointing at the urinal. I always try to find one that looks very similar to a penis. The drunk sees that I am not urinating, and I say, "I'm tired of holding it; here, you hold it," and try to hand the sausage to the drunk. Usually the drunk runs out of the bathroom. I have even had a guy faint on me. It is really funny to see the expression on their faces when I try to hand them my "dick." You can even get a reaction in the school bathroom.

Hot Pepper Juice

You can purchase this by the gallon and use it by the jar. Fill half the victim's coffee cup with hot pepper juice and half with coffee. He or she will really think the coffee is hot. Offer a friend a cola drink and have half filled with pepper juice. Even with ice cubes in his drink, he will feel like his mouth is on fire.

Hoses/Sprinkler Systems

Screw the hose nozzle so that the spraying action stays on. When someone approaches, turn the water on, and the hose will squirt him.

Hook up the sprinkler system and have a friend carry it to the lawn. As he is carrying the sprinkler, turn the water on. He'll get all wet. While the sprinkler is running, pinch the hose so that the water stops. When you dad or friend goes to check out the sprinkler, straighten the hose so the water flows again. The water will come again and wet the same person.

Hide and Scare

All too often this simple prank is overlooked. I get much joy from jumping out and scaring someone. Hide in a corner and wait for someone to walk by and then jump out and say "Gotcha."

While in a bar restroom, grunt and sigh while at the urinal. The drunk will start, look, and gaze and wonder what you are doing.

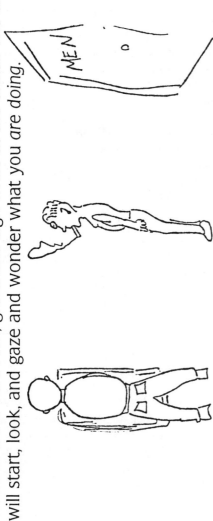

Then turn to him and say, "Here, I'm tired of holding it; take it." He'll move from your sausage fast!

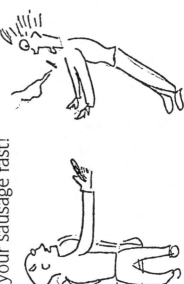

Tell the people in your house that your are leaving. Instead of leaving, hide in the closet and make a knocking sound. The occupants will hear strange noises and be frightened. When they trace the sound to the closet, and the fear heightens, open the door and jump out.

In stores and carry-out groceries, the walk-in cooler is behind the beer, cola, and milk refrigerator. Actually it is all the same. You stock the shelves from the inside of the cooler. Hide inside the cooler and when a customer reaches for a bottle of pop, grab his hand. He'll think the devil got a hold of him, and he'll jump a mile.

I

Ice

During the winter, pick a victim's car and pour a bucket of water over all the doors every half hour. After several buckets, the ice builds up over the car, and it becomes encased in a block of ice. It usually takes the owner all day to chip away the ice to gain entry.

Tell a kid to lick the metal on his sled because it tastes like cheery. But when the kid licks the ice cold metal, his tongue sticks and won't come off. Only warm water will free the tongue from the metal.

Inspector

If you want to get the "royal treatment" in a fast-food establishment, dress respectably and carry a clipboard. Walk around the restaurant and pretend you are checking off items or making a report. The employees will think you are an inspector and try to be super-human in their work. Walk around to the dining tables and ask customers about their meals, look through the windows into the kitchen, and get ready to eat. You will get better service and more food with your order to pacify you. I like to work with a partner on this, because we can verbalize our opinions while writing on our clipboard.

Disappearing Ink

This ink sure can upset someone when it is spilled on a good tablecloth. I like to fumble with a pen and have the ink go all over the place.

While in school, spill it on someone; just when you are about to get in trouble, it has vanished. Write some notes and hope they get confiscated by the teacher. Later, when the evidence is to be used against you, it has evaporated.

Fill your squirt gun with the trick ink and start shooting. Be ready to run because some will be wanting to kill.

J

Jiffy-johns-Porta-potties

Ever go to some outdoor concert or campground and see those rental jiffy-johns? They are deadly fun. I got tired of waiting for this fellow who was taking so long in the rental john, so I got mad and took a stick from the ground, placed it in the outside latches, and locked the fellow in. The person screamed and kicked but couldn't get out. All the people around started laughing, too. From then on I started to carry big 20-penny nails to outdoor events to lock the johns. One person got so angry–he thought by tipping it over, he could get out. It fell over, and he still couldn't get out; all the urine and crap did, however, all over the person inside. It is a hilarious but sick joke to pull, and I had lots of fun with it.

If you have the means to move the john to someone's front lawn, do it. It embarrasses the homeowner, plus he has a very hard time disposing of it.

K

Knockout Drops

These are hard to obtain, illegal, and dangerous, but if you can get them, you'll have a blast. If you give this to a person, zap–he or she is out like a light. Then you can strip the person and dump him on the town square or dress him in girls' clothes. You can paint his body green, yellow, or polka dot. You can do anything.

Keys

If you have the chance to make a spare set of keys to a friend's car, you can drive him crazy. I had a spare set of keys made for my girlfriend's car. When she would park her car to go to class, I would move it to the other end of the parking lot. She'd spend an hour looking for her car. But with the cars getting smaller, a few guys can lift each tire up, slip some rollers under the tires, and roll the car away.

Kotexes, Mini Pads

This is another goodie that your imagination can have fun with. I used to take a Kotex, put a little catsup on it, and place it on my boss's desk. Then when he would get to his desk (usually with an important client in the room), he would have to keep a straight face.

While sitting behind a girl in class, lay it near her books and tell her something just fell out of her purse. She usually leaves the room, too embarrassed to return. This item is fun to have on the school's bulletin board or to tie it to a rear bumper of a car.

When a bunch of us fellows would get together, we would take a box of Kotexes with catsup and a box of rubbers (filled with mushroom sauce) and

While sitting behind a girl in class, secretly place the contraband down by her purse and say loudly, "Sue, something just fell out of your purse."

As she looks and so does the entire class, she'll die of embarrassment!

dump them on the hoods of autos. We'd wait to watch the poor victim try to cope with his mess. It's really hilarious.

When you put a mini pad on the school's bulletin board, write a girl's name on it. Everyone will see it and laugh except the person whose name is on it.

If you are too timid to buy the Kotexes, send me a dollar for each one you want and I'll mail them out to you. My address is in the back of this book.

Tampons

Every time I go to my friend's house, I remove the candles from the holders and replace them with tampons. I remember when his parents were giving a party and went to light the candles; they had a difficult time explaining why a tampon was in there and not a candle. I do this prank every chance I get and have even done it at church. Remember, keep silent to keep from getting caught.

Ku Klux Klan

This is a nasty prank because it makes the victim look like a bigot. Place "Klan Rally" signs in the front yard of your victim, and there's no telling what type of people will show up. Some old college fraternity friends rented a car, placed rally signs on the sides with the mayor's address on them, and drove around town. The school fraternity was angry because the mayor would not issue a permit for a dance. They placed bumper stickers on the victim's car and sent for racist literature in the victims name.

You have to keep a clear perspective on this one, because some actions are illegal, and if you get caught, it can taint your own reputation. When you limit yourself to one race and religion of people you are missing out on a lot of interesting people. Remember, this book is for entertainment reading only.

L

Laxatives

It is hard to get someone to take a laxative without some devious scheming. One of the easiest is to put Ex-Lax in cookies, substituting it for the real chocolate chips; plus, it tastes the same. A bake sale at school is a convenient time to do it. Or, just play the nice guy and give away cookies at school or at work. Tell your friends that you are learning to cook and are asking for constructive criticism. Don't worry if you are a male, because people think it is good that you are developing many interests.

There is also the laxative that is in chewing-gum form. I find this method easier to engineer on people because there is less preparation. Substitute Feenamint in the Chicklet brand of chewing gum and offer it to people. Nearly everyone chews gum so just offer them a couple pieces, and in a few hours they will be beating a path to the toilet. I used to challenge a person to a gum-chewing contest and slip him the laxative gum. The poor fellow never understands why he spends two days in the bathroom. Be sure to mark the gum packs secretly so that you don't get it by mistake.

Letters to the Editor

Nearly every newspaper has an editorial page where citizens can write in and voice their opinion on public matters. The cruel and funny part of this prank is to write a disgusting and stupid letter and sign someone else's name. Let's say you have a grudge against someone and really want to embarrass him to the public. This will work. You can write about how great it is to be an idiot or why cats should wear diapers and then sign the victim's name. Your imagination can run wild and have fun.

You can also write love letters and sign someone else's name to them. I always enjoyed sending a valentine to a married man and signing a girl's name with a note about what a great lover he is. That usually raises quite a stink with the wife.

One of my favorite experiences was when a friend was corresponding with a girl overseas, and we decided to help out. Carl, Ray, Mike, and I did some thinking. I took off my clothes, put on an ape-man mask, and bent over with my head between my legs. Ray took the picture, and Carl and I wrote some kind words on the back. In essence, it said, "Here is a picture of me. Would like a picture of same from you." Carl and Ray went to the post office together to make sure it got mailed. Mike never did hear from that girl. You could use a variation of this prank of a friend's girlfriend.

Locks

Not every student has a lock on his or her school locker, so it's amusing to put locks on selected lockers. The victim can't get into his locker, is late for class, and throws tantrums.

While on the subject of lockers, I usually stack books in such a position that, when the person opens the door, they tumble out all over the floor. This usually makes the person late for class.

License Plates

Take a piece of cardboard the exact size of the license plate so it covers it completely. Make the background color the same as the real plate and the letters the right color, too. Color on renewal stickers the same color as the current year. Try to make it as authentic looking as possible and then do your trickery. Very neatly, letter his plate "I AM GAY" or "I'M STUPID" or anything that would embarrass him if he knew about it. Or, if it's on a girl's car, make a sexual plate. Because it looks so authentic, the victim doesn't notice; however, everyone else does, and they find it just as funny as you.

Lighters

While sitting behind another student in class, take a cigarette lighter and let the flame touch his rump. The victim doesn't know what is happening until his butt feels like it is on fire. He'll scream and jump out of his seat. Everyone will look at him like he is crazy, and of course he'll be embarrassed.

You can take a lighter or blow torch and turn it on the door handle. When someone comes to the door and turns the handle to enter, he'll scream and jump up and down. he will look ridiculous to the other people in the hallway.

On the same order, when all the chairs were taken in our kitchen, someone would have to sit on top of the electric stove. I would secretly push the burner button, and before you know it the victim was jumping for the moon!

The only thing I had on was the ape man mask when I bent over for the picture. Then we sent it to Mike's new girlfriend.

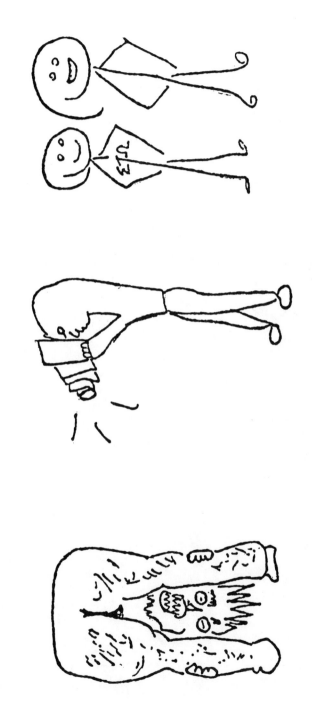

Mike never heard from her after that. He began to think that no girl liked him because they never stayed around.

Foaming Lighter

Seems like you always have someone asking you for a light, not only for cigarettes but everything. I started to carry a commercial foam-shooting lighter and offer it to a victim. When he uses it, the trick light erupts like a volcano, sending foam several feet into the air.

Light bulbs

No one notices light bulbs until they are needed at night. The next time you are left alone at a friend's house, quickly remove all the light bulbs and hide them in a closet. Then, when they go to turn on the lights at night, they all get very frustrated. Every member of the family blames each other, and quite an argument erupts.

Replace the outside porch light with a red bulb. This is a signal for whorehouses. Soon many men will be stopping by to buy some fun. Let's hope your friend doesn't get raided for prostitution.

At night in a dark area, hold a flashlight to the bottom of your chin. When the light is turned on, it distorts your facial features and you will resemble a monster. It is good for scaring youngsters or motorists.

Mice

When a boring class was coming up, I would sneak mice into the room. When the time is right, take them out of the box and let them run loose. The girls start screaming and running. Even the teacher stands on her desk.

If you want to cause a stampede, take the little rodents into a restaurant and watch the women customers run for the doors. Don't laugh until you are down the road; otherwise, you may get thrown out.

Mask

I have already stated what can be done with Halloween masks while driving. Take a mask to school and, when you're outside, pop up in the window. A girl will usually scream, others run. Then it will look like the girl is seeing illusions. I used to do this to the home economics classes.

Now, if you don't have a mask handy, take a jock strap and wear it over your face. Some people may think it's only an air filter. I have also taken undershorts and put them over my face, and this really startles people.

Or, when out on the town at night, chase someone across an intersection with your mask and sheet on.

Movies

I used to get all kinds of looks from people when someone in a movie died and I'd start laughing or just start yelling at the characters. If a horror show was playing and I had seen the movie twice in a row, I'd get up during the scary scene and run screaming out of the theater.

But my favorite, whether at school or the downtown theater, was waiting for a special opportunity to develop. If there is some problem with the film

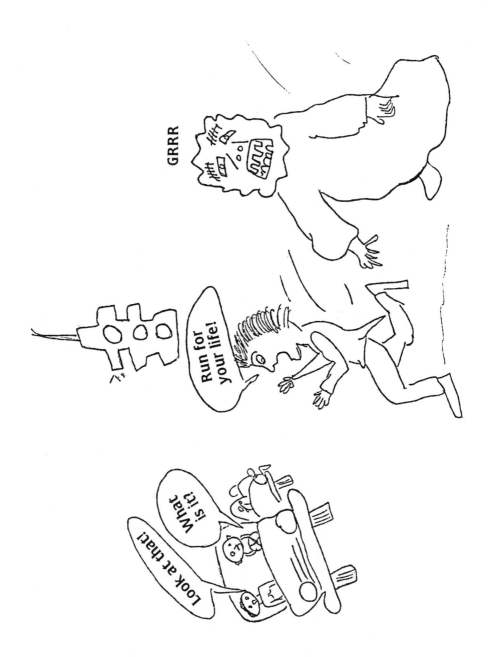

and there is a picture but no sound, jump up with your hands to your ears and shout, "Oh my God, I've gone deaf!"

Paternity Suits

This dirty trick is liable to cause a nervous breakdown for the fellow it's pulled on. That is where my niece came in handy. I would have her call the guy, claim she was pregnant, and say that he was the father and was in real trouble. The fellow couldn't remember because he was drunk and really believed it.

Just have a girl call a fellow and claim that she is three months pregnant and that he better marry her. This can really upset a person, especially if the guy is already married. He is fearful his wife will find out.

Money

People go crazy when they think they are getting free money. A bunch of us fellow would pool our money together and come up with thirty dollars. We would get everything exchanged for one dollar bills. Then we would get a ton of play money and place it in the back seat of our car. We would drive downtown to the university area where there is a multitude of people. We first got everyone's attention and then passed out or threw about five one dollar bills as we slowly drove in the car. Then, as people thought we were throwing out money, we started tossing out the play money. We had real dollars mixed in with the play. People came from everywhere yelling and screaming as they grabbed for the money. They must have thought we had robbed a bank, with all the money coming out of our car windows. People came out of stores and even churches and began to fight over the money. It was a really hilarious.

Shooting the Moon

While driving down the road, pull down your pants and press your bare butt against the rear window. The people in the car behind suddenly see an ugly rump staring them in the face. It's even more comical if three or four people in the rear of your car do it. While stopped at a traffic light, have your friend shoot the moon out the window to the car beside you. Just imagine the answer a parent gives his little girl when asked, "What's that hairy thing hanging on that boy?"

Mix your play money with your real dollars while throwing it out your car windows. People even come running out of church to grab the money!

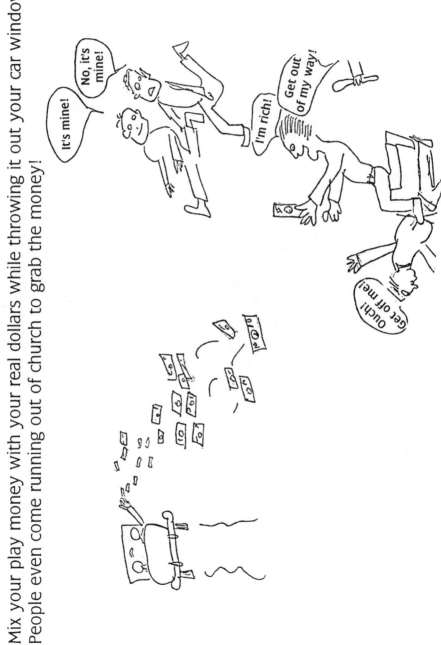

Shoot the moon to pedestrians.

Mustaches

Everyone has a favorite picture on display in his or her house. If the picture is of a person, quickly take it out of the case and pencil in a mustache. When visitors see it, they'll chuckle and get a kick out of it. If you fear you'll ruin the picture and get into trouble, tape on the mustache and get a similar effect. At a public display of posters, just go wild. However, keep it clean and not obscene!

N

Notes

While sitting in class or study hall, a friend and I would write a fictitious note. We would address it to one girl from another. For example "Julie: while my parents were gone, John stayed every night and he forced me to have sex. I missed my period and think I am pregnant. Darlene." When writing this note, include real names of two people dating at your school. Include some additional chit-chat.

I would usually write the note, fold it up, and toss it under the table close to someone. The patsy discovers the note, his eyes get big, and he starts passing it around the room. Soon the note and false rumor are all around the school.

I moved around often when I was younger. I would leave some notes at my friends' houses inviting them to come over. What I failed to mention was that I had moved, and they would go to my old address. Carl was shocked when he tried to walk in the door and found another family there.

Notes for teachers can embarrass them. We would write love notes to male teachers asking them to meet somewhere. We would not sign a girls' name. We would let them guess. We would hide to see if the teacher really would show up.

Nail Polish

After you've gotten some fellow too drunk to know what is going on, paint his fingernails pink. When he wakes up, he'll be astonished. He can't get it off, either, without special remover. You can do this to a sleeping friend who stays all night with you or to someone sleeping in a study hall.

Numbness

Anyone who has had Novocaine injections for dental work knows his or her speech is slurred and he or she just can't talk correctly. It is because the mouth is numb and just doesn't work properly. When a person is drinking a liquid, the liquid just dribbles out of the lips. Anbesol is a product used to stop sore gums or tooth aches. It is easily accessible at any drug store. Mix this liquid in a person's food and after a few bites the person's mouth is completely numb, no feeling. Food starts falling out of his mouth and his speech is slurred. It's pretty funny because the victim has no control until it wears off.

O

Ordering

Go into a fast food restaurant with your friend to order some food. Both of you go to the counter at the same time, because your friend will have to act as your interpreter. When the person asks what you want, you speak in a fake foreign language. Your friend will then translate. For example,
 Waitress: Can I take your order?
 You: Hink Hum tom.
 Friend: He'll have a Coke.
 You: Funda Pond.
 Friend: And a burger and fries.
 The waitress really won't know what to think. She'll just have to take your order. Remember to keep a straight face until you leave the restaurant and then you can roll on the ground.

P

Paper Clips

While sitting in a study hall or classroom, bend a paper clip so that it forms a hook. Then take a rubber band and spread it between your thumb and index finger to form a makeshift slingshot. When shooting the paper clip from your hand, aim high. I always aim at a picture on a wall across the room. be very careful not to hit anyone. It could really hurt someone, even blind him. When the clips start hitting the wall, no one will be able to see where they come from.

Parking Tickets

Don't you get angry when some idiot parks so close to your car you can barely get in? I always try to park away from everyone else, but when I come out of a store there's always someone's car next to mine. For a while I purchased some funny fake parking tickets from a novelty company, but they just didn't have the impact I wanted, so I had some cards printed up that really are nasty. They can really make that person feel like an idiot.

If this card fits your style and you want to order some, just contact me. Ten for $5.00.

> Thanks Assface!
> FOR PARKING SO CLOSE
> NEXT TIME LEAVE A CAN OPENER
> SO I CAN GET MY CAR OUT
> Stupid __?__ like you should
> Ride the --damn Bus!!!

Also, switching legal parking tickets on different cars can cause an exciting situation. The victim won't know what's happening until he's on his way to jail.

Parties

I have to admit this is a very cruel prank, but humorous. Mail out about twenty to thirty party invitations to people you know. Pick an unsuspecting victim and place his or her name and address on the invitation. Then, when the date comes, this person suddenly has twenty people showing up, unan- nounced, to be fed and entertained. the poor host will have a nervous breakdown before the night is over.

I don't know if you can classify this as a practical joke or not. The next time you have a party and the people get a little drunk, have three or four fellows or gals get under a separate blanket for a game. you can get under the blanket, too, to make it look more real. Then tell them they have sixty seconds to throw off what they least need to win a prize. You can act like you are taking your pants off while pants, bras, and everything else is coming off. Some will be nude before ten seconds are up. Then just flip off the blanket and say that it is the least needed item. It works!

Pennies

If you are in a big study hall or class and want to cause some excitement, it only costs a penny. Just lean over like you're reading and then quickly toss the penny over your shoulder. Clang, bang, clang. It catches everyone by surprise, especially the teacher. You must keep a straight face so as not to get suspected.

Personal Pagers

Personal pagers are the little communication box-like devices that, when you dial a specific telephone number, your voice sounds through the gadget to give the message. When boss used to go get a haircut or any other place away from the phone, he would take the pager. I would wait a while to make sure he was with other people, like at the barber shop, and dial the number. Then I would say, "Wow, you really stink. Don't you ever shower?" The voice would come from the little box and really embarrass him. It is under his clothing, like sport coat or sweater, it sounds like he's talking. One can go to check about renting one and get all the telephone numbers for the pager. Just say you'll have to think about it as a way to get out of it. Then start calling all those pagers and voicing your ludicrous remarks.

Read: Act like you are
Look: For teachers
Toss: Pennies over opposite shoulder
Read: Act again
Act: Surprised!

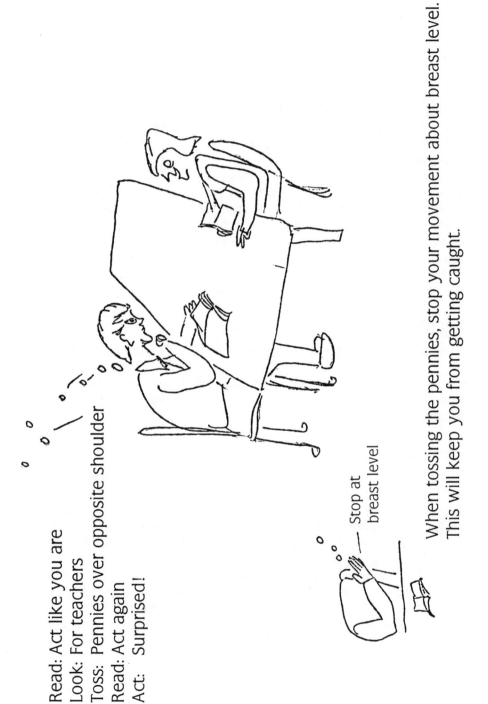

Stop at breast level

When tossing the pennies, stop your movement about breast level. This will keep you from getting caught.

Picket

After a couple had toilet-papered my house, it was time to pull a Devious Dennis. I had several biker buddies picket in front of my victim's house. The signs were not slanderous or dirty, only embarrassing:

"John Doe lives here"

"It happened to me, be careful"

The wife was extremely embarrassed. The neighbors all came outside, and the cops were called, but couldn't do a thing. Remember: keep it clean so there's no hard feelings

Pictures

Most people do not have a photo lab to pull off this prank, but even the crudest method gets results. I used to take a picture of my teacher's face and place it on top of one of a nude body. Then take the combination and pin it on the bulletin board. I even progressed to taking a photo of the picture I made up and "retouching" it, and it would look very authentic. By taking a male face photo and putting on top of a woman, then taking a picture, you can make him look like a transsexual. When an old girlfriend would make me angry, I would do this little photo number on her. I would go up to her new boyfriend and ask, "Do you have any naked pictures of Sue?" Of course he says no. Then you say, "Do you want to buy any?" Well, he thinks you are joking until you pull out your doctored" photos of her.

Pie

Start chasing a friend down a hall with a pie in your hand, ready to hit him. While passing the same people two or three times, pick out a victim to smear. Then, with everyone thinking you are after your friend, hit someone else and run like the devil. The victim is so startled, and, with the pie in his face, he can't chase you. You may want to wear a ski mask to conceal your identity.

Ask a friend to hold someone so you can hit him with a pie. Have everything worked out so each guy knows his job. But what the fellow holding the apparent victim doesn't know is that the victim bends down, and the pie goes in the stooge's face.

A person can make some money by being hired to throw pies in the other people's faces. Just charge $25.00 a hit, and you'll be driving a Cadillac in a year.

When a friend orders a pie, tell him it smells sour or that it may not be safe to eat. When the friend bends his nose down close to smell it, push his face down into the pie. It smears all over his face, making him look foolish. It works best with banana cream pie or any fluffy type. You can try it with cake, too.

Pizza Ads

This is one of my favorites. Photocopy hundreds of Bob's Pizza ads. Make the ad too good to be true so that everyone will want to order large pizzas with everything: $1.50, free delivery, open until 3:30 A.M. Then put your principal's phone number, or that of the head of the university, or of your girlfriend, or of anyone you want to get even with. Pass these out on all the parked cars all over the city. The person will receive phone calls every minute of the day and night. Just look at my example and make yours.

Pizza Calls

Many pizza shops make home deliveries and ask very little information on the phone. It's possible to call a pizza shop and order for a house that really didn't order it. We used to pick a different teacher each weekend. We would call a shop and give the teacher's name and address. Soon the pizza would arrive, and even though the victim did not order it, he would go ahead and take it. However, when you call forty-five or fifty pizza shops and have them deliver to the same house, that is when the fun begins. Park close to the house so you can see a delivery car pull up every five minutes. Be sure to call all the shops at the same time.

Peanut Butter

I have found peanut butter can be a lot of fun and not just for eating. One year my fraternity brother Phil and I were keeping a spare apartment just to take all our women to. Well, Carl was hogging the place with the same girl, and Phil and I were getting disturbed about it. Phil and I got drunk while Carl was out on a date, and I took some chunky peanut butter and smeared it on the toilet seat. It looked just like someone crapped on the seat. Really horrendous, but funny as hell. Phil passed out on the couch, and I went to spend the night at my mother's. Carl came home with his date, and she had to go to the bathroom so badly she was ready to bust. When she went running into the bathroom, Phil woke up in time to hear her scream and lose it because the seat was messed up. Carl called my house at 2:00 A.M. but my Mom answered the phone. Carl said, "Why did Dennis put peanut butter on the commode seat?" Mom said, "Because he's a rotten and crazy kid," and hung up. Over the next month, we used ten jars of peanut butter by smearing it on toilet seats in schools, bowling alleys, etc. Just stand at the urinal and wait for the victim to get sick as he goes into the toilet stall.

Pee

Next time you are showering with the guys, ask one if you ever piss him off. If he says no, then turn towards him and start urinating on his leg. It's okay, because it washes off while you are showering. After a game or gym class, while a bunch of fellows are showering, we pick one fellow and start urinating on his legs.

At fraternity stag shows, Mike was always too lazy to get his own beer refilled, and we would take his cup for him. It would be filled with 20 percent beer, and the other eighty percent would be piss. Yes, that's right, and he never complained. When we would have a chug contest, we would chill some pee to sneak into the contest. Pick a victim to give it to then see who can drink his beer down the fastest. After the first swallow, the victim spits it out, while we roll on the floor with laughter.

Pop-out Items

I don't care how long this simple prank has been around–someone always gets tricked by it. Of all the pop-out tricks, the nut can is my favorite. A hungry person will grab for the can of nuts only to be shocked out of his chair.

Don't forget the old reliable frog and toad. Even as an adult I place a toad in a container so that when a person opens the lid, out jumps the toad. I have found the toad is usually as frightened as the person, because it urinates when jumping from the can.

I like to sneak a rubber worm into my sandwich at school. While eating I have the worm into pop into sight. As I pull the worm out with my finger, I say, "What is this?" Everyone looks at the worm and gets a little sick. I usually carry the worms to the trash can in plain view.

Pinch

One thing Russ and I loved to do when we were in his MG was to pull close beside a girl walking near the road. I would lean out and grab the girl on the butt. The first time I asked Russ to slow down even with traffic behind us, I surprised him with my grabby hand. Soon we got pretty good at it. Really catches the girl off guard. I loved to do this on Christmas and during Spring breaks down in Florida. The streets are full of easy prey.

Another fun grab at school or anywhere is when a girl is walking up the stairs head of you and two other fellows are walking beside you. Then reach out and grab her butt and pull your hand back fast. This way she doesn't know who did it. Also, keep a straight face. She doesn't know whether to slap you or kiss you. It's fun.

Pinchy-winchy

At a party, separate four people from the rest of the crowd. Keep them isolated until it is their turn to play a game involving a stooge. Have everyone stand in a circle and have some lipstick concealed in your hand. The aim of the game is to have everyone do what you do. Pinch the person to your right on the chin, and he continues the chain. But he doesn't realize you just smeared red lipstick on his chin. Everyone else sees this except him. Then you say, "Pinchy-winchy on the nose" and smear it on his nose. Well, the victim goes through the same movement on the next person but without the mess. The victim does the same movement as you. This gets everyone laughing until the victim figures out what's going on.

Pill

While in college I advanced from other forms of contraception to the pill, when I would throw the packet under a girl's seat and tell her something fell out of her purse. I collected all my girlfriend's pill containers, so I had an abundance for a while.

Pockets

How would you like to put your hands in your pockets to get your keys and instead get chopped liver? Sabotage someone's pockets by putting anything gooey in them. I have dumped in jars of Vaseline, chopped liver, anything to shock the person. On small children, I used to put cigarette butts in their pickets so that when their parents checked them, they got in trouble. For girls of any age I would slip a rubber into the pocket. Whom do you think looked more surprised, the mother who found it or the girl when confronted by the mother?

Popcorn

I have to give this practical joke a triple star rating because of the spectacular reaction it gets and also because my ingenuity of invention never seems to falter.

The next time you go to the movies with your girlfriend, buy some popcorn. Because it's fairly dark, you can pull this stunt off fairly easily.

After the popcorn is nearly half empty, get a "hard on" and stick your penis up through the bottom of the box so it is in the popcorn. Then, while holding tightly onto the box, ask your date if she would like some more popcorn. When she reaches in and feels your dick instead, she jumps about a foot out of her seat, thoroughly surprised. I think this is one of the most fun tricks to play. It is really funny. But remember to hold tightly to the box, because she

Your girlfriend will be so surprised when she reaches in the popcorn box that words cannot be uttered!

Just change the name of the victim and phone number and the person you want to be getting a million calls after midnight will be in business.

may accidently pull the box, getting her hand out so quickly that the box could cut you. I learned the hard way.

If you don't think you can do this without her seeing you, put a coat over your lap or ask your girl to go get you something to drink and then do your penetration bit.

Parades

My cousin contacted me to do a practical joke on a former girlfriend of his. He wanted to really embarrass her with a good "Devious Dennis" style of prank. His town was having its annual parade and the victim always went with her family and friends to watch it. I had him enter his pickup truck as a "fruit company" to be in the procession with the entries. We placed sideboards on the truck bed that were nearly chest high. As the parade started, the signs were turned around so that they had the girl's name, address, and phone number on the posters. Essentially it read as: "Jane Doe's Nudist Club... 555 Welcome Drive...555-1212" and the slogan, "Experience the Fantasy." The driver of the truck only had cutoff shorts on and was bare-chested so he appeared nude. The guys in the truck bed had shorts on, but no tops, so with the sideboards, they looked nude. We had a girl in the truck with a towel wrapped around her top so she also gave the appearance of being nude. We went to a discount store and purchased a large quantity of undershorts. As we drove in the parade, the crowd was surprised to see an advertisement for the (fake) nudist club. The crowd was stunned as we threw underwear from the back of the truck saying, "We don't need this anymore!"

When we approached the spot where the victim was sitting watching the parade with her friends, the excitement increased. When she saw the float with her name advertising a nudist club, she was so embarrassed she screamed and ran. Her friends teased her for several weeks.

R

Rabies

Smear whipped cream around a dog's mouth and yell "MAD DOG!" People will look at the dog, think he has rabies, and start running.

Road Blocks

Most construction sites have the bright orange pylon to keep motorists from hitting the men working. Our gang would quickly grab the pylons to use later. We would set up our own road block right in the middle of a main street. We also had the white lumber signs to close off the road. If we ran out of the legitimate materials, we just place blocks, rocks, tree limbs, etc. in the road to stop traffic. Be ready to run from the police, because they are sure to be called.

Rats

One of my most memorable pranks was with my good friend Russ. He was getting ready to leave for mortuary school, so I went to see him the night before he was to leave. I had killed a rat earlier that day in my field and put it in a small paper bag. I concealed it in my jacket and went to his house. We were in his bedroom, and I asked him to go get us a beer for our last drink together. While he was gone I opened his suitcase and stuck my paper bag right in the center. He never suspected a thing. The next day he arrived at an estate where he was to stay as a guest. His parents and host were in the room when he was unpacking and came to the bag. "Mom, Dad, you got me a going-away present." As he emptied the bag, the hostess fainted, and he yelled "Dennis!" His mother said, "Dennis would never do anything like that." Ha ha!

You can go that route, or you can place a dead rat in one of those fast-food hamburger containers. Tell some people you are working with that you bought one burger too many and hand it to someone as you are still eating. Watch that person turn pale and grow weak. You could just leave one lying around in a restaurant, if you have a grudge against the owner. Also, put it in the glove box of someone's car.

Rubbers

Just mentioning this word can cause embarrassment to most people. At school we would lay them on the teacher's desk just to see what his or her reaction would be. Sometimes we would pin them to the bulletin board. Another favorite is to put them on the car antenna or car door handle. I really would get a kick out of slipping one into a girl's purse and then accusing her of carrying some contraband or saying I wanted my letter back. Then I'd force her to dump her purse in front of everyone. They would usually shriek with horror. Another dirty trick would be to leave it in its package and, while sitting behind a girl, carefully place it near her books or purse. Then in a loud voice say, "Something just fell from your purse." By this time everyone is looking at her while she picks up the little packet and gets red in the face. I used to enjoy laying one in someone's plate in the cafeteria or at a restaurant. At a bar, slip a rubber into a person's beer mug when he isn't looking. His reaction will cause everyone to look. If you want to add a little spice to this prank, just put some Ivory dishwashing fluid or cream of mushroom soup down into the end of the rubber, and it will be more disgusting.

If you are too timid to go buy some rubbers, just send me one dollar for each one you want. I'll mail them out to you. My address is in the back.

Railroads

Anytime one deals with railroads, it is potentially dangerous. That's why you should have several guys with you on this prank to help keep watch.

About one hundred feet from the crossing is a trip switch that sets the red lights flashing. Usually this flashing stops cars, and if there are gates, they come down to stop the cars from crossing the tracks. This prank is better if done at night so that people can't see you on the tracks. Have a big light that resembles a train light as the flashers go off. This is realistic. If you want to go one step further, make a locomotive from cardboard and push your train over the crossing while the motorists watch. This really pisses them off, but who cares: if they can't take a joke, screw them!

Railroad Crossing

While everyone is waiting on a train to pass at a crossing, the cars are pointed towards the train. But if you want to embarrass your date or just get a reaction from people, cross the tracks and stop. Your car will be facing the opposite direction of the other cars, with the train behind you. When the train is gone, start the car and drive away, the same as the other motorists but in the opposite direction.

Roman Candles

This is a dangerous item to play with, so be careful if you try this prank. I find it fascinating to place roman candles on opposite sides of the road at railroad crossings. Quickly light the fuses and run to your observation point. Beautifully colored fireballs criss-cross over the motorists. Some hurry across, others are too frightened. It really is a spectacular sight, especially when the flashing lights of a police car arrive.

I like to stick the roman candles on the grill of my car and drive down the street with fireballs shooting from my car. Most people pull off the road and let you have it all to yourself.

Rocks

Many destructive pranks can be devised involving the rock, but it's more fun when no one gets injured. Place rocks in someone's hubcaps of their car and it really makes a terrible clang. It sounds like the car is falling apart, but the driver has a hard time finding what is wrong because every time he stops to find out what is wrong, the clang stops too.

Restrooms

I have written more concerning this prank in the "toilet" section. Changing the "Men" and "Women" signs on the restroom doors can really cause some loud screams. Just imagine a woman without her dress, fixing her girdle, and in walks a man. This usually works best at a school function, when strangers are unfamiliar with the surroundings. You can have authentic looking cardboard signs covering the real ones and after someone enters, take off the fake sign. This makes it easy for an unsuspecting victim to enter wrongly.

After a woman enters the restroom, give her time to get planted on the john. Then quickly open the door and throw a couple of mice in. Listen for the screams and then watch her come running out with her panties still around her ankles.

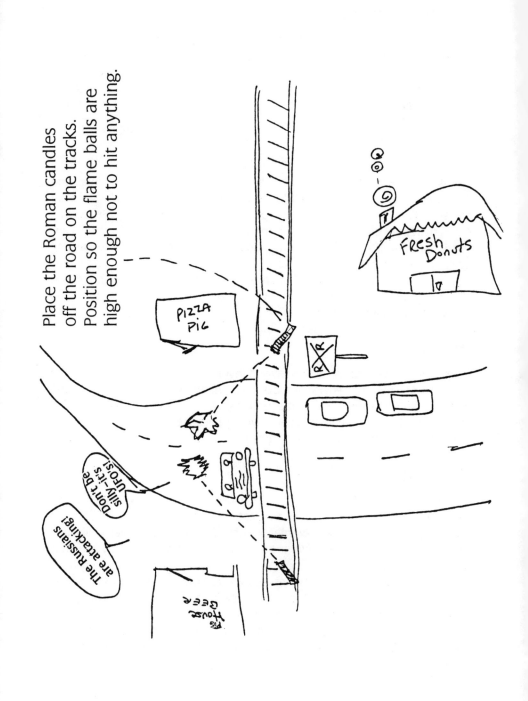
Place the Roman candles off the road on the tracks. Position so the flame balls are high enough not to hit anything.

S

Skeletons

You should be able to purchase fake human skeleton from a novelty magazine. I purchased mine from a scientific catalog and it looks authentic. One of the pranks we would do is have the skeleton lying in a ditch along the roadway. We would flag down a motorist to ask for help regarding our grizzly discovery. Although horrified, they went to contact the authorities. As soon as they left we headed for the closest bar.

At night we would wait along a rural road not far from a cemetery for a passing motorist. As one approached we would stand near the road in black robes with a shovel, pick axe, and our skeleton. It appeared to the motorist that we were grave robbing. Some of the motorists nearly ran off the road in panic.

Snaps

These exploding fun snaps can really catch people off guard. Secretly toss one down behind someone and watch them jump from the loud bang. Lay some of these snaps down in the aisle of a store and watch from a concealed area. When the victims innocently steps on them while walking they get so embarrassed from this loud noise. They feel and look foolish. When a friend would get a new car I would hide the snaps under the tires so that when driving away they heard a loud noise. Also when I do this I place some oil in a squirt gun and shoot the oil onto the engine. It drips down to the pavement and it appears that the vehicle is having mechanical problems. For the next few days I continue to squirt oil on the engine, but stop using the snaps. The victim starts taking the car back to the new car dealership and wants it repaired. The mechanic finally gets tired of this lunatic showing up because there is nothing wrong with the car.

Shaving Cream

I used to wait for an opportunity when a friend would fall asleep while watching television. I would take shaving cream and lather up his hand, then I'd tickle his nose with a string until he couldn't stand it and would grab for his nose. Gosh! The cream would then be all over his face, and he would wake up startled and foolish-looking.

While on the sleeping pranks, you might also paint the victim's face with watercolors. Don't tell him. As he starts walking around, he'll get funny looks from everyone and wonder why. Try to get the victim to got to the store for you in that silly condition. Just imagine how he will feel when he sees his reflection in a store window.

I like to put a sleeping person's hand into a pail of warm water. Sometimes this makes the person wet his pants. How will he explain it to everyone? He can't. Besides, you'll be so busy laughing you won't hear him.

Every once in a while I like to buy that commercial shaving cream gag that is in a can. The victim sprays a dab in his hand to sample, but it won't stop. It just pours out, and before long there is a mountain of cream in the room. There is no way the victim can stop it. Be sure to do it at his house and not at yours, because it is messy.

Soap

Who says you have to wait until Halloween to soap windows? I do it year-round and enjoy it. No one expects it during February, and there is less chance of getting caught.

Take some sucker soap to your friend's house or to the school shower. This soap is really plastic and doesn't do a thing. The person tries to wash but gets no lather. I enjoy the black soap more. A victim starts washing, but a black dye forms and really makes a mess. Even the red soap makes the person thinks he's cut his skin.

Salt

Remove all the sugar from its container and replace with salt. The victim keeps putting in tablespoons, but his drink doesn't get any sweeter. He'll put three spoonfuls in and take a big drink and spit it out all over the table.

If salt is put on the yard, it will kill the grass in any form it's distributed. It will go undetected and is easier if you dilute the salt in water; it will go further. Then take the bucket of water and pour a swastika, a dirty word, or anything. Then, in a day or two, the grass will die in that shape. Anyone who drives by the house will see the embarrassing mark. The owner will have to hide it in some way.

Remove the lid from the salt and place it on the bottom of the shaker. When tilting the shaker upside down, use your hand or paper to keep your salt from spilling out. Now it is ready for your victim.

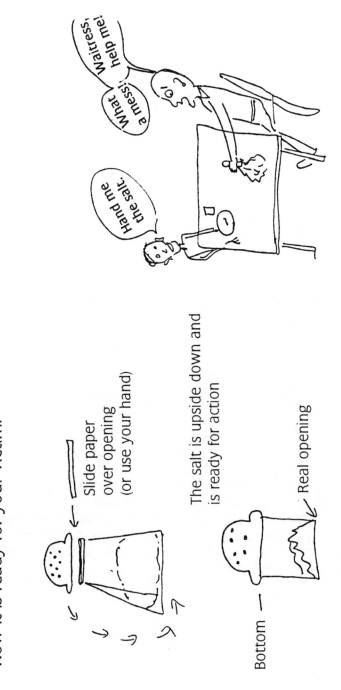

Salt shakers in restaurants are an item for fun. Just take the lid off the top and tip it upside down, holding the salt so it doesn't all fall out. Scoot it across the table to its proper place then set the top on it, and it's ready to go. The next person to use it spills it all over the table. This is also good in the school cafeteria.

Shoe Polish

Everyone has used polish at one time on his or her shoes. It's easy although messy at times. My girlfriend and I used to visit my cousin's car every weekend at work. While it was parked in the parking lot, we used to write all over it some very embarrassing slogans like, "I'm queer. I'm fun to be near," etc. What's nice is that it wipes off without damaging the paint. It's just like at weddings when you write slogans of the honeymoon. But why wait 'til weddings? The person getting into the car is so frustrated he could cry, and we laugh until we ache.

Study Hall

Once you have read this book, more ideas will come to you, but in the meanwhile I'll share this one with you. In a quiet study hall, say, so the teacher can't see you. "Give me liberty or give me death." Keep saying it until she says, "Who said that?" and answer, "Patrick Henry, you dumb shit."

While the victim isn't looking, move his books from under his table to half way across the room. When the period or class is over, the person spends half an hour looking for his property.

Snow

When your selected victim parks his car at work, school, or at the movies, get all your accomplices to help bury his car with snow. Leave the antenna or roof exposed so he can find it; it will take him all night to dig it out.

Many people still believe in legends such as "Big Foot", the "Abominable Snowman" and the like. Cut large animal-monster feet patterns out of plywood, strap them onto your feet, and walk around in the snow. When people see these monster footprints in snow, it will frighten them, and the rumors of the legend will come alive. Even call your newspaper or radio station to get the story going.

Sinks

Most household sinks have the black hose nozzle along with the regular faucet. When the hose is pressed to work, it cancels the water in the faucet. While over at a friend's house, take enough rubber bands to depress the button. When a person turns on the water to get a drink, he'll get soaking wet from the sabotaged hose. Just think: if the mother is the first one to use the water, someone is going to get whacked.

Unscrew the base of the spigot, but make it look as if nothing has been tampered with. When the water is turned on, the spigot flies off, and water shoots up to the ceiling and everywhere else.

Remove the bottom drain pipe of a sink in the school or public restroom. When someone goes to wash his hands, the water goes down the drain but shoots out all over the victim's pants and shoes. It looks as if the victim wet his own pants.

Sausage

If you fellows want to impress some girls or just startle some teachers, stick a foot-long sausage down your pant leg. You'll look so well endowed that maybe you'll get asked out. Act like there is nothing wrong, and no teacher will have the nerve to ask what's down your pants. It looks like a giant hard-on that will impress everyone.

Or, if you have occasion to wear an apron such as in a bachelor's class or as a grocery clerk, this will excite some people. Tie a sausage or knockwurst to a string and put the string through your belt loop. Then when a person gets near, move your apron so that the dangly knockwurst shows. Some timid lady will think you are exposed and faint.

Sleeping Bags

After a person has fallen asleep in the bag, attach a rope to the bag and toss it up over a tree limb and then pull on the rope; the bag will be suspended in mid-air.

Shock Items

I have always enjoyed using the commercial shock book, radio, and pen. Hand the book to a person and watch him jump as he opens the cover. I always ask a victim for his address and hand him the shocking pen for excitement.

If you have vandals sabotaging your car, this plan could stop them in their tracks. Hook a separate car battery to your car so that when anyone touches it, he gets the shock of his life.

Loosen the kitchen spout handle, but don't take it off. When the victim turns on the water for a drink, he gets drowned. It's like a volcano erupting.

Loosen the fitting on the kitchen spout.

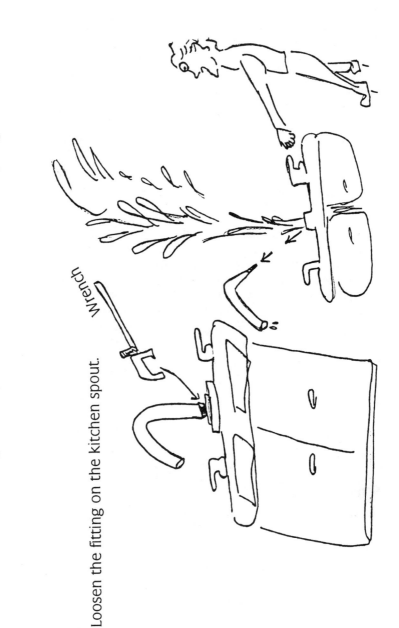

Wrap a rubber band around the nozzle on hose at the kitchen sink; when the water is turned on, the victim will get soaking wet.

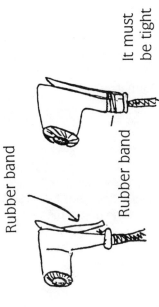

Rubber band

It must be tight

Rubber band

The victim gets a face full of water

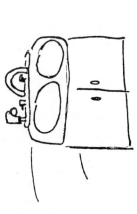

Shit, Manure, Poop, or Whatever You Want to Call It; The Results "R" the Same

I used to take manure, cat's or dog's, or whatever is handiest and put it in a coffee can and secure the lid. Wrap it up in party paper and let it sit and ferment a couple of days. When a person has a birthday, leave it so he will find it around a crowd of people. I did this to Dave at the college lab and at work. But I really did a job when I left it for Ray and signed his old girlfriend's name. It is so funny to watch everyone gather around as the victim unwraps the package. When the lid comes off and the terrible smell flows out, watch everyone run. Sign someone else's name to take the heat off of yourself. If you don't have access to manure, when you go to the bathroom, take good aim and cap the lid. If you're desperate, do it–the laughs are worth it.

Also, place the manure in a paper bag on someone's porch and set the paper bag on fire. The homeowner will come out to stomp out the fire and get the poop all over his foot.

Or, just get a wheelbarrow full of manure and dump it on someone's porch.

The next time you go on a picnic, take along some of the phony bird mess and place it on someone's sandwich. How disgusting. His whole appetite is ruined! This inexpensive trick is well worth its weight in gold.

Spanish Fly

If you are able to get any of this you'll have a blast. However, it is dangerous and illegal, so be discreet in whom you tell. It only takes a drop in a drink or food, and that person will be so horny he or she will attack anything on two legs. Try it at school, a party, or in teacher's drink; she'll start scratching her crotch and getting amorous with the first male that comes along. It also has the same effect on men, so they will attack anything on two legs, even the ugliest of uglies.

Skunks

It's nearly impossible to handle a live wild skunk, because you will get sprayed. If you have the opportunity to get one just killed on the highway, get it to the school ventilation system as soon as possible. I had a de-scented skunk that I used for pranks. I would sneak it into my school class, and people would start jumping out of windows to keep from getting sprayed.

Placing dog crap in a paper sack and setting it on fire may be generations old, but it still works!

For the goon who won't leave your girlfriend alone, I would stink up his car so no female would ride in it. I would fill his car full of manure from the local farmer.

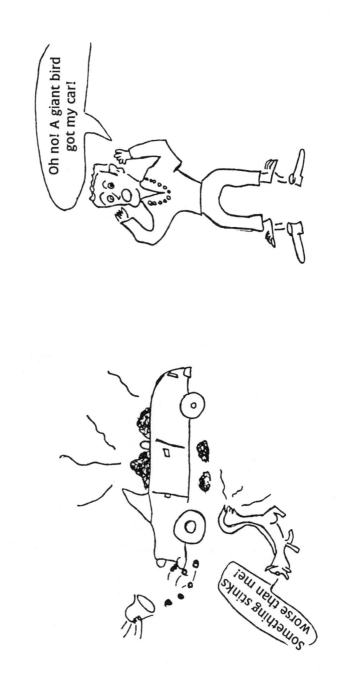

Showers

We used to conspire against a lone fellow in the locker room, and it worked every time. We would wait until a fellow was in the shower and then steal his clothes. We would all disappear but leave him a dress. The only thing he could do was either come to class naked or in a dress. Either way, the fellow lost out. Try it. It's not hard to get the other fellows to go along with you.

At a mixed party of boys and girls, the shower or bath tub can be a fun place. If girls have to use the same restroom, just hide in the shower stall with the curtain pulled to conceal you. When a girl is finally seated on the toilet, casually come out of the shower and surprise her. She'll be so defenseless–she can't stand up or run, just sit there and be exposed. If no shower, hide in the tub. Hide under towels, if needed, to conceal yourself. I find it works more easily if it is a drinking party, but I have pulled it off at sober ones too.

You really won't need a catchy line to get her attention, although you *may* say something like, "Are you voting this year?"

While a person is taking a shower, grab a glass of ice-cold water and quickly throw it on the victim and listen to him scream. It works just as well in a bathtub.

My buddy was upset because his sister kept showing nude baby pictures to his girlfriends. When we knew Beth, his sister, was going to shower for a date, we filled the hot water tank up with green dye. We also sprinkled the green dye flakes on her towel. When she started taking her shower, we turned off the lights. When she finished showering, she began screaming. Her mother came running and saw Beth's green body. She began screaming. Neighbors thought someone was being murdered and called the cops. Beth looked like a green martian.

A few years later a criminalistic friend gave me some detection powder. It's invisible until it gets wet. I lightly sprinkled the powder on a guy's steering wheel, door handles, etc. He was trying to date the same girl as I was. The victim rubbed this invisible powder on his hand and face. When he started to sweat, his face and hands turned blue! He looked like a geek. He had no idea this was on his steering wheel and kept touching it and then rubbing his face through the day. He was taken out of circulation and I got the girl. Fluorescein is a chemical that turns bright green when it gets wet. I watched a prankster sprinkle it on concrete at the local swimming pool and people's feet turned a funny color. It's easy to obtain at chemical supply houses.

Sit-Ups

Bet a person it's impossible to do a sit-up blindfolded after spinning around in a circle five times. Tell him it's never been done and that he can't do it because of the balance required. Naturally he will take you up on it, spin around, and lie down to do his sit-ups. Just as he is on his back and ready to sit up, step over his legs, drop your pants and bend over. When the victim comes up, his face goes right into your butt!

Shorts

Many of the short pants people wear come down very easily. While a victim is wearing shorts and talking to people, sneak up behind him and quickly pull his pants down. He'll be so embarrassed, and his pants will be down to his ankles so that he can't chase you.

I like to catch someone off-guard and give him an Indian; some call it a wedgy. Sneak up behind the victim, grab his underwear and try to pull it up to his shoulders. It is such an uncomfortable feeling; your crotch is squeezed and tight. In order to straighten out his shorts, he has to take down his pants. You can do this in a hallway or anywhere, and the victim is uncomfortable until he finds a secluded spot. This works just as well on girls.

Skinny Dipping

Every weekend during the summer nights, we would jump the fence at the local pool and go skinny dipping. I can remember placing some feces on the diving board–Joe got so disgusted when he stepped in it. He had a hard time cleaning it from between his toes.

If we heard that other fellows were going skinny dipping, we would wait until they were in the water and then run and grab their clothes. The victims have to leave in the nude. Always try to wear a mask to hide your identity. It may save you from repercussions.

If you really want to shock the swimmers, even more than just by putting fish in the pool, throw a mannequin into the pool. This mannequin looks so real in the water that people think someone's drowned.

Smoke Bombs

We used to like to light three or four smoke bombs, throw them into an elevator, and push the button for a floor. When it reaches the destination and the door opens, all this smoke rolls out, and people don't know whether to get in or not.

Hide in the shower at a mixed party and wait till a girl gets planted on the commode before making your appearance. What a *surprise!*

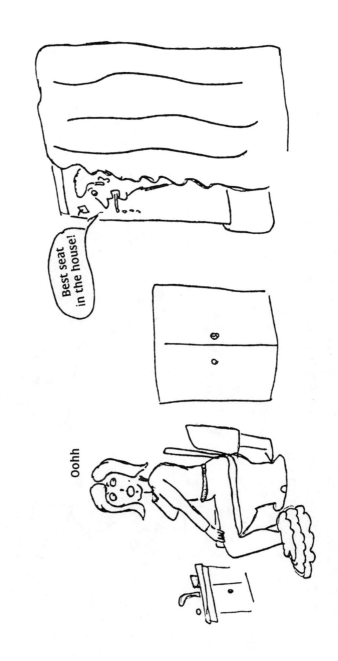

Bet a fellow ten dollars that he can't turn around five times and do a sit-up while blindfolded. Then have your accomplice drop his pants and bend over to catch the victim's face.

I used to like to put delayed smoke bombs in the school restrooms. Also, if you can sneak them into the air ducts at school, everyone gets out for an hour of free time.

For parked cars, conceal them inside the tires so it looks like the car is on fire. Watch the frantic fellow come running out, thinking his car is on fire.

Or, if you want to drive your car and have a smoke shield, place the smoke bombs in tin cans. Hold them outside your window.

Sneeze

I've been to dull parties, boring restaurants, and too-quiet study halls and found the sneeze is a way to liven things up. The teacher will become angry, and you can embarrass your date. Just sneeze and fall off your chair. It surprises everyone.

Snakes

Nearly everyone is afraid of snakes, even the most macho male. If you want to see someone really get excited, throw a couple of snakes in the car. When that person gets in to drive away and a snake wraps around his leg, he won't need the door to get out of the car. The first time I did this was the Mark at work. We couldn't even mention it or we would be fired.

Speed Limit Signs

If you want to see someone get a speeding ticket, just do a number change on the speed limit signs. When a sign says 25 miles an hour, change it to 45. Make a cardboard sign exactly like the real one and post it over the original. Call the police and complain about speeding motorists on that street. The police will post a radar unit and start pulling over the cars.

Snipes

There are still people who have never gone snipe-hunting. Distribute bags to people and tell them that if they go into the woods calling "Snipe," the little animal will come to them. There are some who will search and search but not find anything. You and your buddies can just leave or wait for those foolish people. After an exhausting search, the fools return empty-handed.

Student Drivers

If our gang had a friend or relative taking driving courses, we would get nearby in our car. We had loud speakers and would blast "DANGER, STUDENT DRIVER, GET OFF THE ROAD." The student usually got shook up and parked the car.

We made a sign, "Crash Driving School," and put it on our car with yellow flashing lights. Some motorists would pull off the road when they saw us coming.

Suitcases

Sometimes I think I deserve a pat on the back for my ingenuity, but you readers can just send money. It came about by accident. I was carrying a suitcase around in my car for no actual reason. There were four of us, and we got bored riding around, so I pulled the car off the road and grabbed the suitcase. We went up to the first house we saw, and the rest is history.

Go up to the house and ring the doorbell. When the homeowner comes to the door, say "Here we are! Tell Julie we're here."

Homeowner: "You must have the wrong house."
Joker: "This is the Phillips' residence isn't it?
Homeowner: "Yes."
Joker: "We travelled two hundred miles to get here. She gave us this address and told me to come. It's too far to go back now; what are we going to do?"

Always use the name on the mailbox and keep a straight face. I have had some people invite us in and go through the phone book and call people of the same last name. When you leave, act disappointed. The resident is usually confused but helpful. If you drive, park your car far enough away so they can't see it or get your license number. This is really a lot of fun, and you will discuss each weird experience you encounter. Good luck!

Another suitcase trick is to take a suitcase you don't mind losing and booby-trap the inside. Let a suitcase lie around where someone will be sure to open it up out of curiosity: along the road, in a secluded part of a building, anywhere that you can watch the results. Don't leave any name on the outside; it will cause the victim to open it up just for identification if not for thievery purposes. Then have a spring-action load inside so that, when the lid is opened, something jumps out at the person opening it. You can use a fur object that resembles an animal, or, you can make an animal out of the fur to scare the victim. You'll laugh your head off while you watch someone open the suitcase and jumps for his life as the furry "animal" comes out after him.

Subscriptions

A person gets enough junk mail daily, but how about receiving one hundred unwanted magazines in a weeks' time! I went to the library occasionally and tore out all the mail-in cards for each of the magazines. I must have had over two hundred. Then I put the same person's name on all of them. The poor fellow started receiving so many different publications that he couldn't get

Park your car far enough away or out of sight so that it can't be seen.

rid of them all. Plus, he got the bills to pay for all of them. He was dumbfounded for quite a while.

If you have someone who deserves this fate, just follow my directions. Be sure to include all the dirty magazines. This embarrasses the victim most. Or send all the girly magazines to where they work. This is especially embarrassing for ministers.

Foaming Sugar

I have already discussed sugar tricks, but this foaming sugar is an eye catcher. My uncle thought the tea was too hot and made the sugar foam all over the table. When he took a drink, he spit it out all over the table!

Signs

If you have it in for someone and want to destroy an enemy, here is a sure way. Paint signs on wood or cardboard to embarrass the person. Like "Joe Blow is a crook," or "John Q. Public is a homo." "Becky does it with all the boys." Place the signs on telephone poles, pin them onto buildings, or drive a stake into the ground on his street corner.

Or you can make a sign and tape it onto the back of a person's car; and, while he is driving around, he will never realize that "I suck pony peters" is on his car.

One time our gang was angry at Jeff for some silly reason. We climbed a small mountain with a highway beneath and painted "Jeff is an asshole." It was on the hillside for two years.

One night I was restless, so I got fraternity brothers Bob and Steve out of bed to paint billboards. We painted our fraternity name all over the county.

The next night, Bob, Steve, Phil, and I went to housing projects and painted our slogans on the roofs. Then we moved to inhabited dwellings and did our devious deeds. We got chased by some of the residents and had the law called on us, but it was fun every minute.

Make a sign announcing your friend's birthday and place it on a street corner. However, add ten years to the age on that sign, just for a laugh.

Don't forget the streets. We painted the streets also. We embarrassed a lot of old girlfriends, but who cares?

A lot of times, storeowners will have moveable letters for the outside sign. Just change the letters around to make disgusting words.

Once in a while you see an "Out of Order" sign on a vending machine. Take the "Out of Order" sign off the machine; people will lose their money, kick the machine, and look silly.

Or, just the opposite. Place "Out of Order" signs on all the vending machines, and this will upset the people, too.

Place some grudge signs where they belong–where everyone travels!

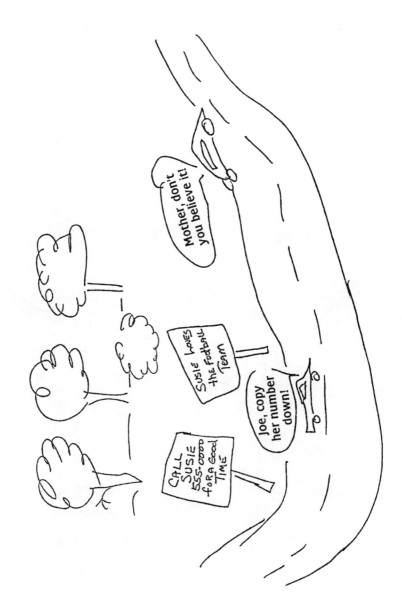

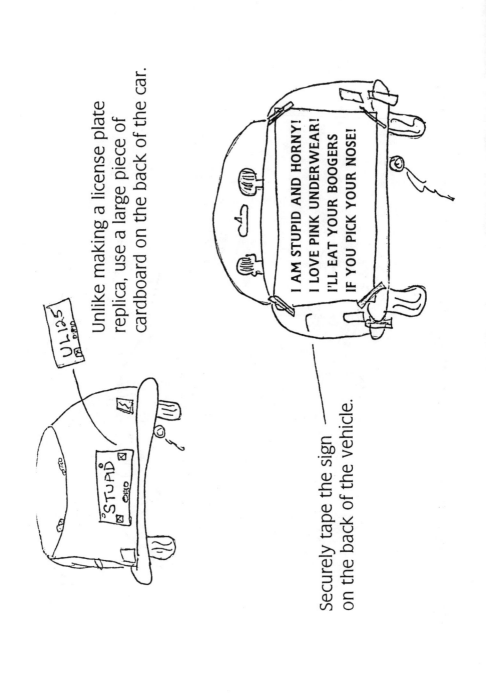

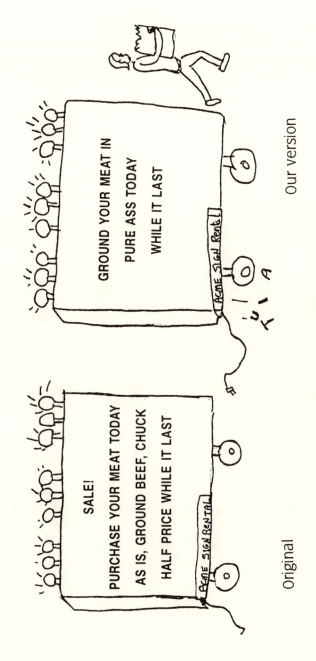

Turn the street signs so the named streets are just the opposite. When a motorist tries to find a house, he is actually on the wrong street.

I would like to caution you not to remove STOP signs. This is very dangerous, and people have been killed by this stupid move. And if you get caught, you get charged with manslaughter. Remember, practical jokes are for fun, not to hurt people seriously.

Make a birthday sign for your friend, but add ten years to his or her age. Then place the sign somewhere on his or her block in plain view.

T

Toothpaste

This is good to do at schools, restroom doors, dormitories, or anywhere a door is closed. Uncap the toothpaste and push the opened end under the closed door so that it points inside the room. Then, step down hard on the tube. This will cause the gooey paste to fly halfway across the room, making a mess. If you remove the tube when finished, the victim will ponder how that mess was made.

Another tasteless joke is to squeeze the paste from the tube gently, then shove a nail back into the tube opening to force the sides outward, making it look full again. Now take white liquid glue, pour it into the toothpaste tube, and recap. When the victim starts to brush his teeth, the fun begins–he may never want to clean his teeth again.

Squeeze some toothpaste along the edge of the sink so that, when a victim leans over it, paste gets all over the victim's clothes.

Teeth

If you have a set of false teeth you don't need, you can put them in the most unusual places. I've slipped them into a bowl of soup; when the person got to the bottom, he got sick. Just laying them on the dinner table will startle people. Tell them you may need an extra pair of teeth to eat. I have even taken a piece of meat and pre-chewed it with the false teeth. Then I stick the meat in my mouth and chew and swallow. The other customers are ready to send me to the funny farm.

To get attention, take black chewing gum and stick it over your front tooth. From a distance, it looks like teeth are missing and is very distracting.

I also got enjoyment from the commercial vampire teeth and goofy teeth you can buy from the novelty catalogue. I would secretly stick the teeth in while walking down the hall with my girlfriend, and she couldn't figure out why we were getting weird looks from others. While in study hall or church, I would secretly stick the teeth in my mouth and smile at someone. It would catch the person off guard, and he'd laugh and be reprimanded.

Tabasco Sauce

You know that tabasco sauce is hot, but you can get the *extremely* hot stuff that is available. It's fun to sneak the sauce into a catsup container and watch the victim go running for a bucket of water. It's fairly easy to substitute at school or at a party. Don't laugh too loud, or they'll figure you did it.

Fake Twenties

Have you ever seen people try to hide the fact that they are picking up money? I printed some fake twenty-dollar bills, folded in half, to scatter around. It's funny to watch people at a carnival or in a public place quickly pick up this twenty and be embarrassed when they read the inside. Some quickly put their foot on it to hide it, and then they look around, quickly stoop and pick it up. If you are with a gang of fellows, you can't keep from going into hysterics.

Fake Trip

The fake trip is when you click heels while walking and fall. You look clumsy while stumbling. This trick goes with the egg trick described earlier. I used to do this when dressed in a three-piece suit while working in funeral homes. Even though you look silly, it is fun.

Trees

Once it gets dark, start chopping on a tree. You have to be quiet, or neighbors will call the police. Chop a little bit each night and pick up the chips to avoid detection. You might place a dark covering over the chop marks to conceal your deed. When you are ready, make the final chops and let the tree fall across the street for an instant roadblock. Then run like hell.

Telephones

One of my favorite calls is to the bowling alley. When the fellow answers, ask "Do you have twenty-pound balls?" He'll say "Yes." Then come back with "Doesn't it hurt when you walk?"

All kinds of gimmicks can result from the phone. Maybe you can devise some new phrases.

Have your friend get on the extension phone at your house and pretend that you are lovers, talking. At the same time, dial a random number. When that person answers, tell him the line is busy and talk intimately to your partner. Lots of confusion develops for the victim.

Call your friend and, when the family goes to get him, hang up. He'll think they tricked him.

If you are with your friend and you need to call someone, tell him you'll dial but he has to speak, because you are embarrassed or have a sore throat. When you dial the number, dial his house so that his parents answer. It will really catch him off guard.

Call up bars and ask for Frank. "Frank who?" asks the bartender, and you'll answer "Frank Furter, isn't that a hot one!" "Is Hairy there?" "Hairy who?" says the bartender. "Hairy Chest, you dimwit," and hang up. The list is endless, and so is the fun you will have.

Tired of getting wrong numbers? If some fellow asks for Julie, I say "Yes, but she never wants to see you again. She is with Mark," and then hang up. Or "Bob got fired yesterday and is looking for a job." Let your imagination run wild. This next incident happens once in a lifetime to one in ten million people, but because of my deviousness, it worked out–I swear. A wrong number called one night and asked for Pam. I said "No, won't I do?" Well, we got to talking; both of us got excited, and she wanted to meet me. I was on call for the ambulance company, but I told her to meet me in forty-five minutes. I drove down to the ambulance company to get the personal pager. I told my partner, Keith, to call me exactly at 10:00 P.M. and say we have a code 89. A code 89 wasn't anything. If she turned out to be a dog, I had an excuse to leave. It turned out to be one of the weirdest and most enjoyable scoring nights. I was with her all that week.

All you need is a little guts and a flair for fun, and you can pull anything off. You have to take chances to win.

You can conduct fake surveys over the phone that lead into sexually related questions. Or, if you want information over the phone, just say you are a Fed, and people will open up to you. One thing to remember: impersonating a federal agent will get you twenty years–if you are caught.

Call someone on the phone and tell him you are the phone company. Explain that you are doing work on the phone wires and tell him not to pick the phone up for three minutes; say it is because the lineman may get shocked and that he will be able to hear other conversations. The person hangs up, but you stay on the phone. Usually the other person is nervy and picks up the receiver to listen to the conversation. When he does, make a buzzing sound, scream, and hang up. The other person will think you were electrocuted.

Place some Vaseline, lard, or shaving cream on the earpiece of a phone. When the phone rings and the victim places the receiver to his ear, he gets an earful of grease. This is very effective at the office, because you can go into the next room and dial. At home, smear the slime on, go to your extension phone, and dial the special number (directions in phone book) that will make your own phone ring. When you smear the mess on the earpiece, make sure its not so sloppy that the victim can see it before it gets crammed in his ear.

This idea involves a tape recorder. Record your questions fast or slow and then play the tape on the phone. If the words are fast, you sound like a munchkin. If slow, you sound like a corpse. Have your dialogue all recorded, leaving limited space for the other person's answer. This takes some planning but can be pulled off.

This one doesn't take planning–only opportunity. If you have extension phones in your house, wait until your brother or sister is talking to a prospective date. Get on the phone in the other room and let a horrendous burp into the phone. It will sound like your brother did it. and he'll be so embarrassed. If you are fast with words, when the two people on the line pause, quickly interject "I can't wait to see you on the toilet." Then run, because if your brother or sister catches you, you are as good as dead.

Tie

Some people have very dull senses. While someone is sitting in study hall or sleeping, tie his shoes together. When the victim gets up to walk, he falls flat on his face.

The commercially purchased pop-up tie is a great gag. The next time you sing in the school choir and wear a tie, do this gag. Have your trick tie creep up into the air. Everyone's eyes will be on you and laughing. The teacher will be so annoyed but helpless.

Tacks

This isn't very original, but it's reliable. Before a class starts, go through the room and place tacks on most of the seats. Place one on the teacher's as well as on your own chair and spot it just as you are sitting down. If you remark upon it, it will usually take the blame off you.

Toilets

Imaginations can run wild with this item. I like to take those little packets of catsup or mustard, tear off the end, roll up, and place underneath the notches of the seat. When someone sits down, he puts pressure on the packet forcing it out as he sits down on the seat. What a surprise! If the red catsup gets on the underwear, it'll look like someone is having her period. She'll be too

While in the restroom, place a camera over the top of the commode stall. Get the person to look up and then take his picture. Don't let him see your face. Then hang the picture on the bulletin board.

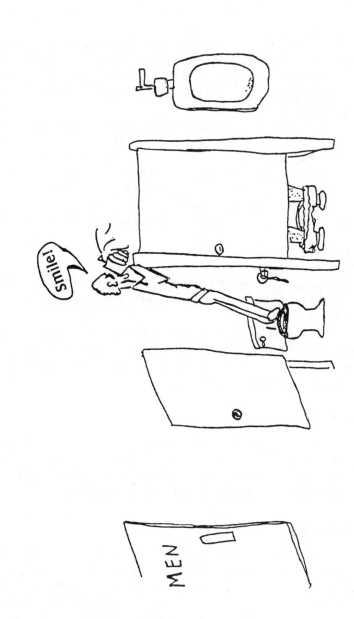

embarrassed to go out. I like to be in the restroom combing my hair so I hear the reaction.

At school I liked to take a camera into the restroom and, when someone was sitting on the john, sneak into the next stall with the camera. Place the camera over the top and take a couple of snapshots then offer to sell them back to the victim for $5.00. I made fifty dollars in one day. Sometimes I would then pin the picture on the bulletin board for laughs.

We used to take old commodes and place them on a homeowner's front lawn just to embarrass him.

We used to go into department stores (not in our hometown), and one of us would go to the different style of toilets and sit down in public. We would discuss the level of comfort. Sometimes we would strip to our undershorts and sit with a book. Yes, we did get thrown out, but the people around us were completely dumbfounded.

When someone is on the toilet in a stall, take a glass of cold water, throw it over the top of the stall, and run out of the restroom. This is terrific at schools and public restrooms.

If you want to buy those gimmicks out of novelty books, they're okay, but I like to rely on my own devious intellect to invent pranks. You can buy those squirt devices or talking devices, but they can only be used in your own home or else you'll lose them.

Take clear cellophane wrap and, with the lid raised, spread it smoothly across the bowl. Then lower the seat and you're in business. When a woman sits down to tinkle, it splashes back on her and makes a mess of her bottom.

In a public or school restroom, stuff toilet paper or some obstructive material down the toilet, out of sight. When the toilet is flushed, it overflows and makes a mess. Remember not to do it at your own house.

When a person has to go to a public restroom, his is usually desperate. I used to go into the bathroom stall and lock the door. Then crawl under the stall into the next one, close the door, and lock it. All the stall doors are locked, and no one can get in. Wait in the restroom, combing your hair, and wait for some desperate person to try to get to use the commode. He'll try pushing on every door and end up crawling underneath the door.

To gross someone out, take buckets of manure, be it horse, cow, or whatever, and dump them into the commode. Fill the toilet until the manure just peeks out of the seat. Lay a piece of toilet tissue on top, and it'll look like someone just couldn't stop defecating.

U

Urinals

This has to be one of my favorite pranks. When I was at school or at work, I used to take a pipe wrench and loosen the fittings on the urinals. When you loosen the nuts on the pipes, the urinal squirts water every time it is flushed. The victim standing in front of the urinal gets his pants soaking wet. He is so embarrassed that he could cry, and I laugh hysterically while combing my hair in the mirror. The poor fellow is too embarrassed to leave.

I used to buy those fake urinals in novelty catalogues and take them to parties. The fake urinal sticks to the wall via adhesive suction. When a fellow goes into the bathroom, either at public places or in private homes, that's when the fun begins. Poke a hole in the bottom so that as he is tinkling, it is trickling onto the floor. He doesn't know what to do! Does he clean it up or just float away in shock?

I've taken a person's picture and put it in the urinal and waited to see the reaction of that person when he comes into the men's room. But, if you want an immediate reaction, take a dollar bill, or a five or a ten; the higher the denomination, the more the temptation. Place the bill in the urinal. Then hang around in the boys room to see if anyone has enough courage to take the bill out. A guy would really like to reach down and take that five dollar bill out, but with someone standing next to them, he won't.

UFO

Have several people call the authorities to tell them they spotted a UFO. If enough people call nightly claiming they saw a UFO, the community gets national attention. You can make giant burn marks in a field to resemble a saucer shape. This can be very convincing and make people believe that one landed. Be careful when scorching the earth that you don't cause any forest

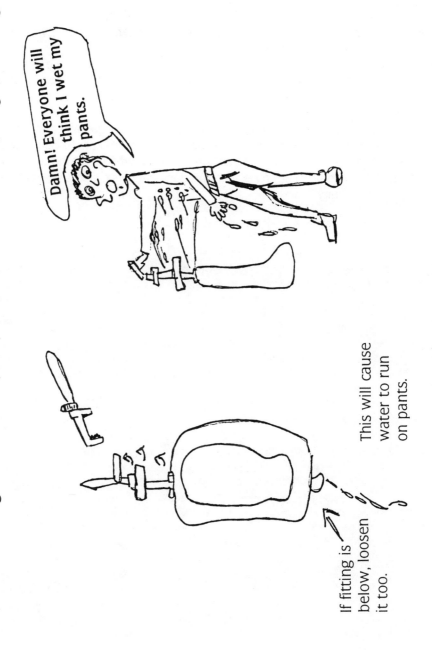

fires. I had a friend who went as far as making tape recordings of space ships and giving them to the media. People were afraid to go out at night for weeks.

You can also fill balloons (the bigger the better) with helium and coat them with florescent paint. Weight them with bricks so they don't float out of the atmosphere. At night the balloon will be very visible because it glows in darkness. And, when you paint spaceship designs on it, people will be sure to call authorities to report a UFO.

While all the UFO sightings are being called in, dress up like spacemen. When people see Martians along the road, it will cause a public panic. Don't stay out so much that people realize it's a hoax. Do it in rural areas, the county roads, any isolated spots.

If you have plenty of money to spend, rent a helicopter and clamp a giant saucer-shaped object beneath equipped with flashing lights. Have loud speakers making spaceship sounds. This sound system drowns out the copter noise and is very convincing. I have seen this done only once, and it sent panic into the community.

V

Vaseline

I love to smear this thinly over the toilet seat, and, when the person goes to sit, he or she slides right off. My girlfriend really hit the floor hard because she was in a hurry.

Once over at my friend's house, I smeared it, but nothing happened. The next morning he called me to say he'd just slid off. I finally knew my deed was complete.

You can also smear it on door handles. I like to watch the teacher's face when he grabs the classroom doorknob and slips off. Don't laugh, or he'll know you did it.

Vomit

It's fun to buy that store-bought plastic vomit or fake dog mess and say that someone was sick. At school or work, lay the vomit on the desk and watch people's stomachs turn.

But, if you want to get out of class or just gross people out, here's how. Take a clear, leakproof plastic bag and put chunks of food and liquid in it. Stick it down the front of your shirt so that the opening can be pulled over your collar. In the appropriate place (classroom, gymnasium, party, car, street corner, or bus), bend over and start making gagging noises. Then, while bent over, apply pressure on the bag: it looks like the food is coming out of your mouth. To make people sick, do it by the window of a restaurant or in the school cafeteria.

Lightly smear some petroleum jelly on your victim's toilet seat so it can't be seen. When he is in a hurry, he slides off right onto the floor. I always carry a jar when I go visiting.

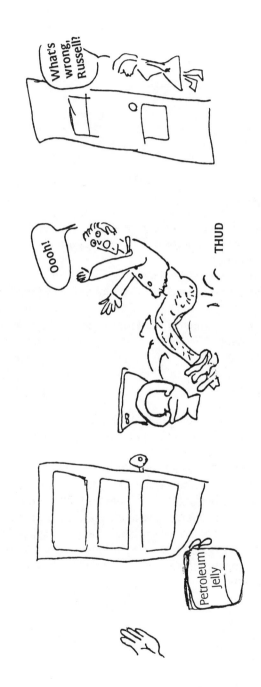

Valentine

I already discussed this in the section about Letters. But, if you exchange valentines at school, write words of love on the card and sign someone else's name. I find it more disgusting to put a few pubic hairs and dirty words in the card. Mail this to a married couple, and someone gets in hot water.

Vodka

This clear, odorless liquid can be used to get someone zapped without his or her knowing it.

At the office or Nautilus shop, they usually have bottle water. Mix in the vodka and watch them act silly.

You can mix it into a cola and get those enlightening results. You can also cut out the end of a watermelon and empty a bottle of vodka into it.

One of my favorite situations is to put vodka in the coffeemaker. Our secretary, who is only a two-cup person, drank six and was dancing on her desk by noon.

If your church uses grape juice at communion, pour in a bottle of vodka before the service begins. If you can substitute some cheap wine, it is even better. All the parishioners will start choking as soon as they take a drink.

Voodoo

Many people are superstitious and are frightened of the unknown. Mold clay into a doll form, or a small doll baby will do for this trick. Stick pins into the doll so it resembles a voodoo curse doll. Get a picture of the victim, stick on the doll, and leave it in places where the victim will find it. The more dolls you make and leave around, the more the victim gets scared. Soon small accidents happen to the victim out of his own clumsiness, and he thinks it's from that stupid doll. Do not send one through the mail, because authorities don't think it is funny.

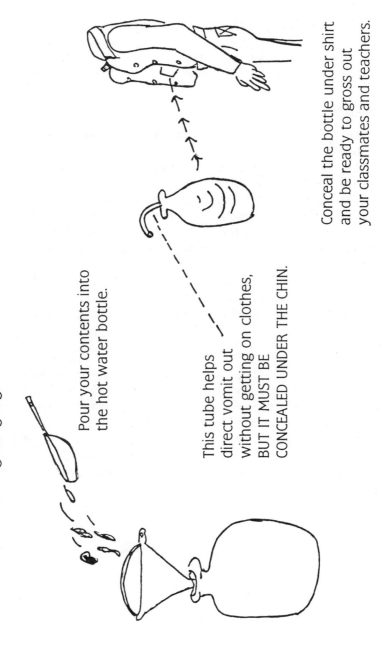

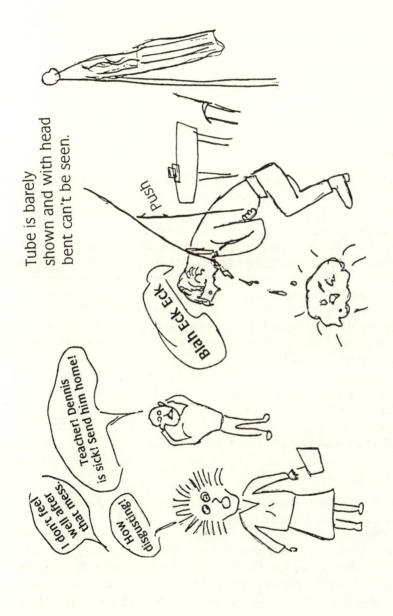

Bend over and push in on the bottle, forcing the "vomit" through the tube and onto the floor.

Walking

If you have the nerve to act goofy alone, more power to you. But when I am with a group of people, I usually walk like I have a physical defect. It really embarrasses the people I am with. I am concerned that I will encounter a real handicapped person, so I don't do it very often.

To get people to notice you, try walking down the street with your arm around a girl while she is secretly holding hands with another boy. It appears that you don't know what is going on and that the girl has a secret lover.

When walking with a group of guys, pick out one you want to embarrass. While walking, just grab his hand so it looks like two boys are holding hands. While you are in a store around other people, say to your buddy, "I'll give up girls and anything if you would be my lover again." That will usually make the person die of embarrassment.

To get attention, open a door and make it appear to hit your head. when opening, place your foot at the bottom so it stops before it hits your head. It sounds like it hits your head and looks that way also. Have a small tomato or catsup container concealed in your hand. Place your hand to your forehead and smear the red on to make it look like an injury.

Bushwhacking

Every community has its lovers' lane where couples go to make out. The fun begins as you and your friends slowly drive up to the lovers's car and turn on the lights and make noise. They usually scramble for their clothes and speed away. Because we knew where all the "parking" spots were, we would hide our car and wait on foot for the lovers to arrive. When they did, we would wait a few minutes to let them get started. We would quietly sneak up to the car and watch. After we got our eyes filled, we would turn on our flashlights and start pecking at the windows and screaming like wild animals. It's really hilarious to watch their reactions. It can be dangerous too! I have had the driver get out and try to fight, and I had to jump in a ditch as one tried to run me down. It's the excitement of life and death situations that usually makes it fun.

A local cemetery was a parking spot for a while until we put on white sheets and acted like ghosts. Both of the lovers were horrified when they thought ghosts were after them in the cemetery. You can also do this while your sister is being kissed goodnight at the door after a date: she will come into the house screaming, and the boyfriend will wet his pants.

Another angle of bushwhacking is to have about six fellows in a car with your and go to a lovers' lane. Drive and park until a car arrives. As it approaches, have everyone in the car get down except the driver and the person next to him. Have them pretend like they are necking. When the car thinks they are bushwhacking you and starts pushing you around, all six of you guys get out and beat the hell out of them.

Water Glass

Again in the restaurant, this little trick can make a big mess. Take a glass of water and put a flat paper surface (a menu will do) on top. Turn the glass upside down holding it so no water spills out. Then, slide it onto the table. Usually a bus person or waitress is in such a hurry that he or she doesn't notice the glass of water as being different. It is nearly undetectable. When it's picked up, the suction lets loose, and water goes everywhere. If new customers have just sat down to be served and the table isn't cleared yet, it is even more hilarious.

Wrecks

Everyone has seen a driver back into a parked car and dent or sideswipe by accident. It's customary for the driver to get out and leave a note on the windshield telling who he is, etc. He has to do it, or some witness will take his license number and he'll get picked up for "hit and run." What I do is similar, but my note is worded differently: "I just hit your car, and the people who witnessed it think I am leaving my name and address on your windshield, but they are wrong. I'm just pretending to do it. Tough luck, buddy."

A similar prank I have fun with is to write a note and place it on the windshield. The note states, "Hey sucker, I just hit your car and damaged it good. Some people think I am leaving my name, but they are as stupid as you. Try and find me, jerk." Naturally, when the owner reads the note, he starts looking his car over for damage. My friends and I have laughed for hours as the poor victim looks for that damage when there is none.

The old restaurant trick still works.

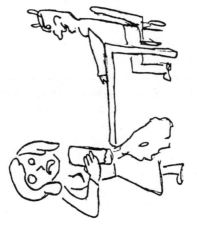

Cardboard or paper must be tight over top so water doesn't leak out.

The waitress gets water all over the place as she clears the table.

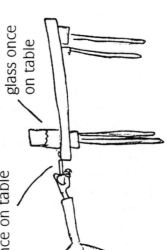

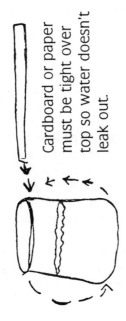

Pull paper out once on table

Can slide glass once on table

Waste Baskets

Everyone knows that if the trash isn't taken outside, it starts to smell. At school we would take garbage from home and stick it in the waste basket. It is much easier to take limburger cheese and throw it into the basket. Soon the room stinks so bad that the teacher evacuates the classroom.

When the custodian tries to empty the basket, he can't because it is full of water. During the course of the day, have every student empty a glass of water into the basket. Cover the water and paper and other trash, and this will conceal the water.

Wieners

I would like to share another fraternity experience that involved hotdogs. For one school event we purchased ten pounds of wieners, but the occasion was canceled due to bad weather. I told Ed to return the hotdogs and get our money back. Ed forgot, and the wieners sat in the trunk of his car more than two weeks before he remembered. We discovered this mishap while at brother Mike's apartment, which was also part of his father's trucking company. We used it unofficially as our meeting place. We took the ten pounds of rotten, moldy wieners and started hiding them in all of Mike's clothes. We stuck one in each piece of underwear, each shirt, pair of pants, and coats. Hid them in his dresser drawers. Placed them in his pillow cases on the bed and in between the covers. Then we placed some in his suits and overcoats. When we exhausted his personal items, we threw some into the toilets and let them stay, (they were gross-looking and couldn't be flushed down the drain). He had to take them out with his hands. Then we put the rest in the typewriter and business files.

After six months had elapsed and everything was cleaned up, I was setting off firecrackers in the apartment with the brothers. Carl pointed to Mike's overcoat, so I stuck a lighted firecracker in the pocket. Boom! Out shot an old wiener like a rocket. We couldn't control our laughter but finally managed to return the hotdog to the pocket. About six months later, Mike and his sister, Judy, took his coat to the dry cleaners. The counter lady went through his pockets and pulled out year-old, moldy wieners. Mike and Judy nearly died of embarrassment. so, you see how such an innocent thing as a hotdog can be a good practical joke; just use your imagination.

Another prank related to hotdogs is that when someone at a party asks for a wiener in a bun, just substitute your own tool and watch the expression. If you don't want to substitute your tool, slide in a rubber hotdog. Everyone will be chewing their wieners, and some poor victim won't be able to understand why his teeth don't penetrate the meat. I have bought several of these trick dogs, because the victim gets disgusted, throws it into the trash, and grabs a new wiener.

Usually at parties, the men are separated from the women for the "leg" game. The men are individually blindfolded and taken to the room of women, and they feel the leg of each woman from the knee down to the foot. The object of the game is for the fellow to guess his partner's knee and win a prize. However, I like a different version of the game. Have all the fellows go into another room and have a large sheet concealing all the men. Cut small holes in the sheet and have each fellow stick a different brand of wiener through the hole. Keep this game a secret from the girls until it's time to play. Take each individual girl into a dark room and tell her she is to pick her boyfriend by seeing only a small part of his body. When she is ready, turn on the lights, and she will think it is the man's real penis sticking through the sheet. She'll be so embarrassed that she may faint. It's good to get a picture of her facial expression to show the other party guests.

The next time you go to the stuffed animal section of the toy department, take some wieners. Position the wiener on a teddy bear or other animal to make it look like its ding dong is hanging out.

But my favorite prank is to go up to a clothed male mannequin (store dummy) and unzip his pants, placing a wiener there. It looks like his ding dong is hanging out, and it's quite comical. Stand back far enough, pretending to look at merchandise but close enough to hear and see comments of other people. Remember not to burst out laughing when a little girl with her mother points and says, "What's that thing hanging on that boy?"

Wires

We really didn't use any wires, but my friend and I would get on opposite sides of a street and wait for a car to approach. As the car got closer, we acted like we were pulling up on a wire so it would entangle the car. The driver usually would stop and, upset about the wire, swear at us. Of course, there is no wire, and the driver really feels foolish when he realizes he go upset over nothing.

Whoopie Cushion

This air-filled balloon can make even the sourpuss laugh. Secretly place on a chair just before someone sits down and when he does, the biggest fart sound comes sending forth. I did this to my teacher once and it took the class the whole day to settle down. When my secretary sat down and farted, she came up off her seat so fast, spilling her coffee all over her desk. It's a lot of fun to watch the victim's face.

I've acquired an electronic whoopie cushion that is remote controlled. One attaches the sound box beneath a chair and from a distance can activate the button so it sounds like the victim is passing gas. In some instances this device is easier to use than the old inflatable cushion. I got rid of a date one time by placing the electronic whoopie cushion in my pocket. While we were waiting to be seated in a restaurant, I asked my date to hold my coat while I went to the restroom. I activated the remote control button and the disgusting sounds erupted. People moved away from by date. She was extremely embarrassed. This incident flustered her more than the time I secretly set her clocks forward an hour, making her early for all of her appointments. I've even attached the electronic cushion beneath the chair of another table in a restaurant. When a patron sits down to eat, the fun begins. The victim's friends usually get embarrassed from the "passing gas" sounds they leave. This also works well to place under the seat in a movie theater. When the lights are dimmed the theater is usually so full so the victim can't move to another seat.

ZOWIE! I WON!!!

I have some friends that enter every contest that exists, especially those "magazine" contests. I went to a professional printer and had authentic looking letterhead and envelopes from a "magazine" company printed for me. In the letter I explained that the person had won $50,000 and that his name was submitted by a mutual friend. I explained that a limousine would be delivering the check on a certain day and time; if they wished to contact friends or the media to be present that would be acceptable. I had some friends rent a limousine and a van. The van pulled up to the victim's house first and got out fake cameras to record as the limo pulled up. There were several people at the house waiting for the check. As the check was being presented the name was read but with the wrong wife's name. When the unsuspecting couple said that the name was incorrect, it was explained that the check and the results of the contest were invalid. The presenter of the check said, "Sorry, rules are rules" and drove off. The victims were so disappointed they began to blame each other and argue. The camera people continued to tape all this and I played it for the losers at my next party.

Since it was expensive renting a limo, I've also tried a different tactic. I just mailed the winners notification and no prize presenter ever appeared. The victims waited outside their home for three hours. Using certified mail makes the winning announcement appear more authentic. You can still video tape it from a parked van or just show up for the event.

My Next Book

I am working on my next practical joke book, and you readers can help me. I want you to submit your dirty tricks and practical jokes, and I will compile and publish them. I will print your name and story, but please use fictional names.

Just see how amazed your friends will act when you show them the new prank book with your name in it. Send me as many contributions as you have experienced.

Also, I am working on an excuse book for being late for work. For example, "I fell asleep on the bus and missed my stop. Please don't fire me." If you want your name and contribution in it, just send it to me.

When ordering, or just submitting material, mail to this address:

Devious Dennis
In care of the Publisher

Getting Rich

Just about everyone can use some extra money. I have grouped together a list of approximately 100 ideas on how to make money. Some of the ideas are simple and require a minimum of labor. With all the choices, you are bound to find something that appeals to you. It's possible to make some good bucks if you work at it. If you send me a self-addressed envelope, I will forward the information back to you. You must have the self-addressed envelope included to get the free packet.

Ordering Information

If you want some information on any story in this book, drop me a line. If you want to know where to get prank articles, comic letters, or a Devious Dennis T-shirt let me know. Also, if you need advice on how to "get even" with an individual, explain your problem and I will order my subordinates to obtain the information for you. Please send a self-addressed envelope with your inquiry.